James Drummond, Joseph Anderson

Ancient scottish weapons

A series of drawings by the late

James Drummond, Joseph Anderson

Ancient scottish weapons
A series of drawings by the late

ISBN/EAN: 9783742857187

Manufactured in Europe, USA, Canada, Australia, Japa

Cover: Foto ©Andreas Hilbeck / pixelio.de

Manufactured and distributed by brebook publishing software
(www.brebook.com)

James Drummond, Joseph Anderson

Ancient scottish weapons

FIVE HUNDRED COPIES
ONLY
PRINTED FOR SALE

OF WHICH THIS IS
N

Ancient Scottish Weapons &c.

A SERIES OF DRAWINGS BY THE LATE

JAMES DRUMMOND, R.S.A.

WITH INTRODUCTION & DESCRIPTIVE NOTES BY

JOSEPH ANDERSON

CUSTODIER OF THE NATIONAL MUSEUM OF ANTIQUITIES
EDINBURGH

GEORGE WATERSTON & SONS

EDINBURGH & LONDON

MDCCCLXXXI

CONTENTS

It was, therefore, a happy inspiration which led Mr Drummond to contemplate the formation of this unique series of drawings. Apart from their intrinsic merits as the products of a pencil specially devoted to the illustration of all that was distinctively national in the history and art of Scotland, the series thus brought together is unexampled in range and variety, and almost completely representative in character. At his death these drawings, with others illustrative of other phases of national art in Scotland, were acquired by the Society of Antiquaries of Scotland, the purchase being effected by the aid of subscriptions from the Fellows of the Society and others, who felt that an opportunity of acquiring a collection so distinctively national should not be allowed to pass without an effort being made to secure its preservation. The drawings themselves are now preserved in the library of the Society as part of the National Museum of the Antiquities of Scotland, with which Mr Drummond had been so long and so intimately connected. The issue of a volume containing Mr Drummond's Drawings of Sculptured Monuments in Iona and the West Highlands having been undertaken by the Society for its subscribing Fellows, the publishers of the present volume applied for and received the permission of the Society to prepare and issue to the public *fac-simile* reproductions of the series of Drawings of Scottish Arms, Implements, and Ornaments, which are now delineated and described in the following pages.

The descriptions of the Plates being necessarily confined to the simplest possible statement of individual characteristics, it has been deemed advisable to prefix a brief sketch of the general historical and other relations of the different classes of objects, including some notices of Highland Dress and Armour, which are necessary to give completeness and consistency to the summary, and to embody Mr Drummond's views on these subjects.

THE HIGHLAND DRESS.

The first historical notice of the distinctive character of the Highland dress is found in the Icelandic Sagas. When the death of Malcolm Canmore plunged Scotland into anarchy, Magnus Olafson, the king of Norway, was engaged in ravaging the western coasts, and securing a firmer hold of the Hebrides for the kingdom of Norway. On his return from that expedition, in 1093, the Sagas relate that he adopted the costume of these western lands; and they add that he and his followers "went about bare-legged, having short kirtles and upper wraps, and so men called him Barelegs."

But the precise form of the dress at this early period is not more distinctly indicated, and its component parts are nowhere more minutely specified.[*] On the early sculptured monuments of the Celtic period there are representations of lay and clerical dress, but the sculptures are weather-worn and indistinct, and the details are treated in a highly conventional manner. For instance, a kilt-like dress is shown on the monuments at Drainie, Kirriemuir, Dupplin, and St Andrews; a plaid-like upper wrap is seen on the monuments at Hilton of Cadboll, Drainie, and St Andrews; a dress resembling the plaid and trews is on one of the monuments at Kirriemuir, and a jerkin and trews on the monument at Golspie. These are the only representations of the Celtic dress which

---

[*] The historical authorities for the dress and armour of the Highlands are collected, and the subject fully discussed in the ninth chapter of "The Highlanders of Scotland, their Origin, History, and Antiquities, &c." by W. F. Skene. London, 1837. "The Costume of the Clans," by John Sobieski and Charles Stuart, 1845, was a sumptuous book for its time, but requires to be used with caution.

come near the time when King Magnus, by his adoption of a costume which was unfamiliar in Norway, acquired among his countrymen the distinctive epithet of Barelegs.

John Major, in his History [*] written in 1512, describes the dress of the Highlanders of his day in much the same terms as the Sagas, applying to a period five centuries earlier. He says that they have no covering for the leg from the middle of the thigh to the foot, and that they clothe themselves with a mantle instead of an upper garment, and a shirt dyed with saffron.

When King James V. made a hunting expedition into the Highlands in 1538, a Highland dress was provided for the occasion,[†] and the accounts of the Lord High Treasurer show that it consisted of a "short Heland coit," hose of "tertane," and a "syde," *i.e.*, an unusually long shirt:—

> "ITEM, in the first for ij elnis ane quarter elne of variant cullorit velvet to be the Kingis Grace ane schort Heland coit, price of the elne vj[lb.] summa . . . . xiij[lb.] x[s]
> ITEM for iij elnis, quarter elne of grene taffatyis to lyne the said coit with, price of the elne x[s] summa . . . . xxxiij[s] vj[d]
> ITEM for iij clnes of Heland tertane to be hois to the Kingis Grace, price of the elne iilj[s] iiij[d] summa . . . . xiij[s]
> "ITEM for xv elnis of bolland claith to be syde Heland sarkis to the Kingis Grace, price of the elne viij[s] . . . . vj[lb.]"

John Lesley, Bishop of Ross, writing in 1578, says that the clothing of the Highlanders was made for use, and not for ornament.[‡] Both nobles and common people wore mantles of one sort, the nobles preferring theirs to be of several colours. The rest of their garments consisted of a short woollen jacket with the sleeves open below, and a covering for the thighs of the simplest kind, more for decency than show, or protection from cold. They had linen shirts, which the rich coloured with saffron, while the common people smeared theirs with grease to preserve them longer clean. In their manufacture, ornament and a certain attention to taste were not wanting, and they were very neatly sewed with silk thread, chiefly of a green or red colour.

Buchanan, writing in 1582, states that the colours preferred for the stripes of the variegated stuffs they used for clothing were chiefly purple and blue, but the diversely coloured fabrics which had been formerly common were then falling into disuse, and the common people had mostly brown garments, of the colour of the heather—to the effect that when they lie among the heather, the bright colours of their clothing might not betray them.[§]

John Taylor, the Water Poet, in 1618, says that their habit is shoes with but one sole; stockings, which they call short hose, made of a warm stuff they call tartan, and a jerkin of the same stuff with a plaid about their shoulders, which is a mantle of finer and better stuff; blue flat caps on their heads, and a handkerchief knit with two knots about their neck.[||]

In the "History of Scots Affairs from 1637 to 1641," sometimes attributed to Robert Gordon of Straloch, but written by his son, James Gordon, Parson of Rothiemay, who died in 1686, there was an account of the Highlanders in the first book prefixed to the notice of the battle of Glenlivat. The first book of Gordon's History does not now exist, but this passage is preserved in a fragment

---

* "Historia Majoris Britanniæ, tam Angliæ quam Scotiæ." 4to. Edinburgh, 1740 (Second Edition). p. 36.
† Notices of the Highland Dress and Armour, printed in the Appendix to the Iona Club volume entitled "Collectanea de Rebus Albanicis." Edinburgh, 1839.
‡ "De Origine, Moribus et Rebus Gestis Scotorum." 4to. Romæ, 1578. P. 58.
§ "Rerum Scoticarum Historia." Edinburgh, folio, 1582. P. 8.
|| "The Pennylesse Pilgrimage." Lond. 1633.

of the "Memoirs of Scottish Affairs" by James Man, who has quoted it, with some remarks on its severity.[*] It gives a full description of the Highland dress as follows:—

"As for their apparel, next the skin they wear a short linnen shirt, which the great men among them sometimes dye of saffron colour. They use it short, that it may not encumber them when running or travelling. In the sharp winter weather the Highland men wear close trouzes, which cover the thighs, legs, and feet. To fence their feet they put on Rullions or raw leather shoes. Above their shirt they have a single coat, reaching no further than the navel. Their uppermost garment is a loose cloke of several ells, striped and party-coloured (the tartan plaid), which they gird breadth-wise with a leathern belt so as it scarce covers the knees, and that for the above-mentioned reason, that it may be no lett to them when on a journey or doing any work. For the greatest part of the plaid covers the uppermost parts of the body. Sometimes it is all folded round the body about the region of the belt, for disengaging and leaving the hands free; and sometimes 'tis wrapped round all that is above the flank. The trouzes are for winter use; at other times they content themselves with short hose, which scarce reach to the knee."

Martin, who travelled through the Western Isles about 1700,[†] states that at that time the common people mostly, and persons of distinction generally, wore the garb in fashion in the south of Scotland, consisting of coat, waistcoat, breeches, and blue-bonnet. But he adds that many of the common people continued to wear the trews, although it required more skill to make it than the ordinary habit. The old habit of the belted plaid was also retained for travelling, because it was much easier and lighter than breeches or trews. "The plaid," he says, "is tied round the middle with a leather belt; it is pleated from the belt to the knee very nicely," and fastened in front on the breast with a bodkin of bone or wood.

This is almost exactly the statement of Captain Burt, who says of the Highlanders of the mainland that "few besides gentlemen wear the trews—that is, the breeches and stockings all of one piece, and drawn on together; over this habit they wear a plaid, and the whole garb is made of chequered tartan or plaiding." But he adds that those who travel on foot vary this mode of dress into the kilt, which he thus describes:—A small part of the plaid is set in folds and girt round the waist, to make of it a short petticoat that reaches half-way down the thigh; the rest is brought over the shoulder, and fastened below the neck in front with a bodkin or sharpened piece of stick. In this way of wearing the plaid they have nothing else to cover them, and are often barefoot, but some have shoes made out of a raw cow-hide, with the hair turned outward. "Some I have seen," he says, "which, being ill made, the wearer's foot looked like a rough-footed hen or pigeon." Martin also notices this fashion of shoes, which were simply a piece of the hide of a deer, cow, or horse, with the hair on, and tied behind and before with a point of leather. The manner of making them is quaintly described by John Elder, a Caithness priest, who sent a description of Scotland to Henry VIII. in 1542 or 1543.[‡] He says:—

"Please it your Majestie to understande, that we of all people can tolerat, suffir, and away best with colde, for bothe somir and wynter (excepte when the frost is most vehemente), goynge alwaies bair-leggide and bair-footide, our delite and pleasure is not onely in huntynge of redd deir, wolffes, foxes, and graies, whereof we absounde, and have greate plentie, but also in rynninge, leapinge, swymmynge, shootyngts, and throwing of dartes: therfor, insomuch as we use and delite so to go alwaies, the tendir delicatt gentilmen of Scotland call us Reddshankes.

"And agayne in winter, whene the frost is moste vehement (as I have saide), which we can not suffir bairfootide, so weill as snow, which can never hurt us whene it comes to our girdills, we go a huntynge and after that

* Printed in the "History of Scots Affairs from 1637 to 1641," by James Gordon, parson of Rothiemay. (Spalding Club Edition), vol. I. Appendix to the Preface, p. xliii.

† "Description of the Western Isles." By M. Martin. Second Edition. Lond. 1716, p. 206.

‡ "Collectanea de Rebus Albanicis," p. 28.

we have slayne redd deir, we flaye off the **skyne, by and by,** and settinge of our hair foote on the insyde thereof, for need of cunnynge shoomakers, by **your Graces** pardon, we play the sutters; cumpassinge and mesuringe so much thereof as shall retche up to our **anclers,** prycking the upper part thereof also with holis, that the water may repas when it entres, and **stretchide up with a** strong thwange of the same, meitand above our saidle ancklers, so, and please your noble Grace **we make our shoois;** therfor, we usinge such maner of shoois, the roghe, hairie syde outwart, in your Grace's **dominion of England,** we be callit roghe-footide Scottis."

From such incidental notices and descriptions it may be inferred, though there is no precise testimony on the subject, that there were two varieties of the Highland dress—the belted plaid and the trews; and that of these two the belted plaid was the older and more general and distinctive. This was the conclusion to which Mr Drummond came after an exhaustive examination of all the materials within his reach; and although the general subject of the Highland Dress forms no part of the specific object of the present work, it has been so far alluded to because these views are embraced in a description by him of one of the Powder Horns in his own collection, which was read before the Society of Antiquaries of Scotland, 8th April 1872. His drawing of the Horn is given in Plate XX. From its intricately engraved monogram he concluded that it had belonged to Sir George Mackenzie of Tarbat, who was born in 1630, and succeeded to the baronetcy in 1654.[*] Assuming that the two figures represented in the hunting scene engraved upon the horn were most probably intended to represent Sir George himself and his gillie, Mr Drummond considered these representations interesting as throwing light upon a vexed question in regard to the Highland dress. "Sir George," he says, "is represented with his gun over his shoulder, and in front of him is a deer-hound held by him in leash. He wears the belted plaid. His attendant is blowing a hunting-horn, and holds the rest for his master's gun. His dress is in every respect different from that of his chief. Sir George is represented as dressed in a slashed jerkin of the time of Charles I.—a vandyke frill and a flat bonnet with a feather, and by his side his powder horn and his dirk. He wears the plaid belted, above the trews, for although a deer-hound stands in front of him, yet his legs are seen above the knees, and *are chequered as far as seen.* Those who believe that the trews were never worn with the belted plaid may think this a mistake of the artist, but this objection is answered by the dress of his attendant, who wears hose, tabbed at the top and worn a good way under the knee, with a jerkin and sporran, but, excepting the hose, with no appearance of tartan." Mr Drummond was undoubtedly right in his conclusion that the trews and belted plaid were worn together, even if this representation on the powder horn should be held to be insufficient evidence. In 1656 Mr Thomas Tucker, in his report upon the settlement of the revenues of Excise and Customs in Scotland, incidentally mentions[†] that one of the collectors in the Highlands, with the view of averting the antipathy of the natives to an exciseman, "went clad after the mode of his country with belted playde, trowses, and brogues." A passage which occurs in a letter from Mr Robert Farquharson, a chaplain in the Earl of Mar's army in 1715,[‡] is equally distinct on this point. He says that after the battle of Killiecrankie "there were severals of the common men that died in the hills, for having cast away their plaids at going into the battle they had not wherewithal to cover them but their shirts;

* There is extant a document dated at Strathpeffer, 15th May 1680, in which Sir George Mackenzie of Tarbat describes himself as "Master of the Game from Lochen to Killiecuig, and from Conan to Portmealy and Hoikel Water," by Commission from Charles II.—"Antiquarian Notes," by C. Fraser Macintosh of Drummond. Inverness, 1865. P. 239.

† "Miscellany of the Burgh Records Society," p. 4.

‡ Cited by Sobieski and Chas. Stuart in "The Costume of the Clans," p. 104. Another letter, cited in the same work (p. 104) states that John Macrae of Invenhiel, being struck in the thigh by a musket shot at Killiecrankie, the wound was difficult to heal, because the ball had carried with it the cloth of his belted plaid and the trews he wore under them.

whereas many of the gentlemen that instead of short hose did wear **trewis** under their belted plaids, though they were sorely pinched, did fare better in their short **coats and** trewis than those that were naked to the belt."

The parson of Rothiemay, **whose** account of the Highland dress **has been** previously quoted, says expressly that "the trowzes **are for winter** use," which implies that the **belted plaid,** which he calls their uppermost garment, **was then worn over** them, "at other times they **content themselves** with short hose." **It is plain also** from Burt's description of the "kilt," or "quelt," **as he spells it,** that it is the belted **plaid he** is speaking of, and not the kilt of the present fashion, from which **the** upper part of the plaid has been disjoined.

The *feile beg*, or "little kilt," appears in formal record for the first time in the Act passed in 1747, prohibiting the wearing of the Highland dress, by which it was enacted that neither man nor boy, except such as should be employed as officers and soldiers, should on any pretence wear or put on the clothes commonly called Highland clothes, viz., the plaid, philibeg or little kilt,[*] trowse, shoulder-belts, or any part whatsoever of what peculiarly belongs to the Highland garb; and that no tartan or party-coloured plaid or stuff should be used for greatcoats or for upper-coats on pain of imprisonment for six months, without the option of a fine, for the first offence, and of transportation for seven years if convicted a second time. Stewart of Garth, describing the dress of the Black Watch embodied at Taybridge in 1740, says:—

"The uniform was a scarlet **jacket and** waistcoat, with buff facings and white lace, tartan plaid of twelve yards plaited round the middle of the body, the upper part being fixed on the left shoulder ready to be thrown loose and wrapped over both shoulders and firelock in rainy weather. At night the plaid served the purpose of a blanket, and was a sufficient covering for the Highlander. These were called belted plaids from being kept tight to the body by a belt, and were worn on guard, reviews, and on all occasions when the men were in full dress. On this belt hung the pistols and dirk when worn. In the barracks, and when not on duty, the *little kilt* or philibeg was worn, a blue bonnet with a border of white, red, and green, arranged in small squares, and a tuft of feathers. The arms were a musket, a bayonet, and a large basket-hilted broadsword. These were furnished by Government; such of the men as chose to supply themselves with pistols and dirks were allowed to carry them, and some had targets after the fashion of the country. The sword-belt was of black leather, and the cartouch-box was carried in front, supported by a narrow belt round the middle.[†]

"There is thus," says Mr Skene, "a complete chain of authorities for the dress of the Highlanders, from the fourteenth to the seventeenth century, having consisted of the Highland shirt stained with saffron, the Breacan or belted plaid, the short Highland coat, and the cuaran or buskins, and that their limbs from the thigh to the ancle were certainly uncovered. . . . The truis cannot be traced in the Highlands previous to the sixteenth century. . . . Among the gentry the plaid was always of tartan, and the coat appears to have been, from 1538, of tartan velvet and slashed; the short hose were likewise of tartan, but the Highland shirt was of linen and dyed with saffron. Among the common people the plaid was certainly not of tartan, but generally brown in colour, while the shirt worn by them was of tartan. The present dress, with the belted plaid, is exactly the same as the old dress of the gentry, with the exception of the yellow shirt. The dress, with the kilt and shoulder plaid, is probably a corruption of the dress of the common people."[‡]

* The invention of the little kilt is ascribed, by a writer in the "Edinburgh Magazine," to two Englishmen, Mr Rawlinson, Manager of the Works of a Liverpool Iron Smelting Company in Glengarry, and Mr Parkinson, an Army Tailor, who was on a visit to the establishment, and saw the inconvenience of the belted-plaid as a working dress. "The problem to be solved was, to make a dress, not higher in price than the belted-plaid, that would retain the plaits and admit of the free use of the limbs when at work. The tailor solved the problem with his shears. He cut off the lower part of the plaid that belted round the loins, and formed permanent plaits in it with the needle—and lo, the kilt! while the upper part, forming the shoulder plaid, could be fastened round the shoulders as before." The story is well told, but, like many well told stories, wants authentication. It is evident that the change arose when the altered circumstances of the people made continuous labour common, and a convenient and inexpensive garb a necessity; but it is not so evident that it required the genius of an army tailor to solve the simple problem.

† "Sketches of the Character, Manners, and present state of the Highlanders of Scotland." Second Edition. Edinburgh, 1822. P. 247.

‡ "The Highlanders of Scotland," Vol. I. pp. 225-233.

HIGHLAND ARMOUR.

In a state of society like that which prevailed in the Highlands, when every man bore arms, defensive armour was a necessary part of the equipment of all who could afford to wear it. But as there was little or no direct communication, in the way of commerce, with the foreign centres of industry in which such costly products as suits of mail or armour of plate were manufactured, the changes in the forms and character of different varieties of defensive armour, which in other countries are distinctive of well defined periods, do not apply to the armour in use among the chiefs of the Highlands. The old forms, once introduced, were retained from necessity, and associated with forms of purely native origin from choice.

Whatever may have been the extent to which Scotland, in general, was dependent on foreign production for the supply of armour of defence, there can be no doubt that there were armourers in most of the principal towns,* and there is no reason for supposing that the exercise of the craft was entirely confined to them. In earlier times the hereditary smiths of the old Celtic polity were sufficient for the requirements of the tribes, and though we have no records to attest the fact, it is highly probable that the repair, and even the fabrication of body armour of iron, was not altogether unknown in the Highlands.

Although the earlier representations on the sculptured monuments of the Celtic period, in Eastern Scotland, afford no certain indications of the use of body armour, there are many monuments in the Western Highlands which exhibit the general character of the armour in use from the fourteenth to the sixteenth centuries.† They show but one variety of head-defence, the camailed bassinet of the high conical pointed form, which is characteristic of the knightly effigies of England of the fourteenth century. The camail falls low over the shoulders, and covers the upper part of the hauberk of mail, which is usually worn with it. The hauberk is long sleeved, close-fitting at the wrist, and reaching usually to the knee, but occasionally to the middle of the calf. In the earlier examples it has a divided skirt. In the later or more elaborately sculptured effigies the sleeves are shown encircled by bands above and below the elbow. In one instance the elbows are covered by finely ornamented coudières of plate. The leg defences appear, in some cases, to be chausses of mail, while in others they seem to be of plate. The feet are usually more defaced than the rest of the figure, but in some instances they appear as if encased in pointed sollerets. In one case, and only one, the figure is represented in complete armour of plate.

It still remains an open question what may have been the material of the upper tunic of defence represented on the effigies. In the earlier figures carved on the slabs in which the upper tunic of defence is represented with a divided skirt, it can scarcely be anything else than the ordinary long-sleeved hauberk of mail. But in most of the recumbent effigies the tunic of defence

---

* The Exchequer Rolls of the reign of David II. contain payments to armourers for the king's armour and tilting armour. Among these there is a payment, in 1364, *pro armaturis*, to the executors of Alexander Johnson of Linlithgow.—"Exchequer Rolls of Scotland," Vol. II. p. 168. Three generations of a family of Moncurs were armourers in Dundee, between 1444 and 1472. James Moncur, *factor armorum*, is mentioned as supplying King James IV. in 1444; William appears from 1454 to 1468; and John in 1472.—"Accounts of the Lord High Treasurer of Scotland," Vol. I. p. clxxx.

† Instances of these monuments, showing different varieties of the body-armour of the period, may be seen in the plates of "The Sculptured Monuments of Iona and the West Highlands," by James Drummond, R.S.A. Folio, 1881. Issued by the Society of Antiquaries of Scotland. And in "The Sculptured Stones of Scotland," by John Stuart, LL.D. (Spalding Club). 2 vols, folio, 1856-1867. Also Captain White's "Archaeological Sketches in Kintyre and Knapdale," 2 vols, folio, 1873-1875.

is represented with a wide undivided skirt, regularly sculptured into longitudinal folds or plaits, which are distinctly suggestive of the appearance of quilting. It is true that the camail or gorget of mail is also represented in these effigies by folds or plaits arranged transversely, but in some cases it is further distinguished from the tunic by rows of punctulations between the folds, which are distinctly suggestive of the appearance of chain-mail. Some of the body defences are represented as tunics which fit more tightly, have less amplitude of skirt, and fewer folds; the sleeves especially and the body of the tunic being represented as smooth in appearance, and thus giving no suggestion of quilting. If these differences be not due to mere conventionality of artistic representation, they may be taken as representing the three varieties of body-armour that were in use in the Highlands—the hauberk of mail, the quilted habergeon of linen or canvass, and the haketon or 'jack' of leather.

John Major, in 1512, describing the armour of the Highlanders, states, that "in time of war they cover their whole body with a shirt of mail of iron rings and fight in that." But he also adds, that the common people "rush into battle having for body-armour a linen tunic manifoldly sewed (i.e. quilted) and painted, or daubed with pitch, with a covering of deerskin. John Lesley, writing about 1578, is more precise. He says, that "for defence they use a coat of mail woven of iron rings which they wear over a leather jerkin, stout and of handsome appearance, which we call an actou." The Act of Parliament, passed under the Regency of Morton in 1574, for a general weaponshowing throughout the kingdom, appoints separate equipments for the Highlands and Lowlands, and directs that the arms in which the Highlanders are to appear at the musters shall be:—" Haberschonis, steil-bonettis, hektonis, swords, bows and dorlochis, or culveringis."

Reverting to Martin's statements that the leni croich or yellow shirt was " the first habit worn by persons of distinction in the islands," and that it "was the upper garb, reaching below the knees, and tied with a belt round the middle;" and taking these statements in connection with the fact that "the ordinary number of ells used to make this robe was twenty-four," it seems evident that it must have been thickly plaited or quilted, and that it corresponds to the "manifoldly sewed and painted garment of linen or canvass," mentioned by John Major, as the common war habit of those who did not possess shirts of mail. Major also mentions the "shirt dyed with saffron" as a part of the ordinary dress, but as he subsequently goes on to describe the defensive-dress used in time of war, of which he states that there were two varieties, one being a shirt of mail of iron rings, and the other a manifoldly sewed and painted garment of linen, it seems clear that there are also two very different varieties of linen garments implied in his description—the one a simple shirt or under-garment dyed with saffron for ordinary wear, and the other a war-shirt or upper-garb, plaited or stuffed and quilted for defence, and worn chiefly by those who had not shirts of mail.* No doubt, as Lesley states, the shirt of mail was often worn over such a quilted tunic or a haketon of leather; but the number who could afford this extravagance of outfit would always be few.

In point of fact there is no instance of the hauberk of mail, represented as worn over one of these quilted suits, among the monuments of the West Highlands. The monumental slab at Kilmartin, which is a fairly typical example of those that show the hauberk with divided skirt,

* Angus, son of Lachlaw Macintosh, chief of Clan Chattan, in an attempt to surprise the castle of Rathven in Badenoch in 1591 or 1592, is described by the anonymous writer of a MS. History of the Gordons, preserved in the Advocates' Library, as "Cloathed in a yellow warr coat which amongst them is the badge of the chieftaines or heads of clans." This can scarcely mean anything but the leni-croich of Martin, or the quilted tunic of painted canvass of John Major.

represents a warrior with a high conical pointed bassinet, to which is attached a camail of mail descending to the shoulders, and passing straight across the upper part of the chest, and a hauberk indistinguishable in texture from the camail, except that at the upper part of the arms there is a

faint appearance of folds or ridges. The hauberk distinctly shows the divided skirt reaching barely to the knee, and the legs exhibit no appearance of *chausses*, though this may be due to the weathered condition of the monument. The right arm shows the sleeve of the hauberk reaching

c

to the wrist. The right hand holds the spear and the left grasps the sword-hilt. The sword has a triangular five-lobed pommel, the lower part rounded, and having its convexity opposed to the convexity of the guard, which is curved towards the point. The sword, as is usual in these West Highland effigies, is represented as thrust obliquely underneath the belt. The recumbent effigy, popularly known as "The M'Quarrie," at St Oran's Chapel, Iona, is a fairly representative example of the type with the longer, wider, and apparently quilted tunic with undivided skirt. It represents a warrior reposing at full length, his head supported by a cushion. He wears the high conical pointed bassinet, more distinctly peaked or ridged than that represented at Kilmartin. The camail also falls lower on the shoulders, and instead of passing straight across the upper part of the chest, comes lower over the breast. The tunic is ridged longitudinally in regular and closely set folds, and differs in texture from the camail, inasmuch as the hollows between the ridges are not punctulated. The presence of this punctulation in the camail gives a distinct suggestion of chain-mail, while the want of it between the folds of the tunic supplies as distinctly a suggestion of quilting. The tunic is longer than the hauberk represented at Kilmartin, and completely covers the knees. The sleeves reach to the wrists and are covered by a gauntleted glove. Two bands are fixed on the arms above and below the elbows. The right hand holds the spear; on the left arm is a heater-shaped shield, the upper part bearing a galley and pennon, and the lower two animals surrounded by a tressure-like bordure. The sword, which is thrust obliquely underneath the belt, has a lozenge-shaped multi-lobed pommel and a reversed guard, the quillons bent angularly towards the point. The legs appear as if encased in *jambs* of plate, and the feet as if protected by pointed *sollerets*.

There is other evidence which goes far to show that this upper tunic, which is thus sculptured on the West Highland monuments, was not of mail. In the Abbey of Roscommon there is an altar-shaped tomb which Sir W. R. Wilde has identified as that of Felim, son of Cathal Crovederg O'Conor, King of Connaught, who died and is recorded to have been interred in the Abbey in 1265. The front of the tomb is decorated by sculptured figures of armed men.[*] They wear the same high conical peaked bassinets, with camails falling low on the breast in front, over short-sleeved hauberks of mail reaching to the knee. The sleeves of the hauberk terminate at the elbow, and show the sleeves of a quilted tunic, the skirt of which falls some inches below the skirt of the hauberk, and reaches below the knee. The quilted folds are as strongly marked, in the portions that are not concealed by the hauberk, as they are on the West Highland effigies.

Spenser, in his "View of Ireland," refers to the quilted leathern jack as worn universally by the Galloglasses, even at home and in time of peace. Martin alludes to the *Galloglach* of the Western Isles, but limits the term to the personal attendants of the chiefs, who formed a kind of body-guard in time of war.[†] It seems probable, that while the chiefs themselves may have worn hauberks of mail, with or without the jack or haketon, their Galloglasses or personal retainers would be accoutred in the quilted harness only, and the general body of their followers would be

---

[*] Two of these figures are engraved by Sir W. R. Wilde, in his Memoir of Gabriel Beranger, in the "Journal of the Royal Historical and Archaeological Association of Ireland." Vol. I. Fourth Series. 1870-71. P. 252.

[†] Shakspeare knew the term and what was implied in it—

"The merciless Macdonald
(Worthy to be a rebel, for to that
The multiplying villanies of nature
Do swarm upon him) from the Western Isles
Of Kerns and Galloglasses is supplied."
                            MACBETH, *Act I. sc. 2.*

armed each according to his means and station. This is curiously illustrated by the accompanying photo-lithograph from a drawing by Albrecht Durer, preserved in the British Museum, which gives characteristic representations of the dress, armour, arms, and equipment of the gentlemen and their retainers of the early part of the sixteenth century. The drawing bears the initials A. D. as a monogram, under the date 1521, and shows two groups of figures in the armour and costume of the period. Over the first group is the inscription :—

Also gand dij krigs man in Irlandia hindter Engeland.

In this wise go the warriors (war-men) in Ireland beyond England.

And over the second group another inscription :—

Allso gand dij pawren in Irlandia.

In this wise go the poor men in Ireland.

The foremost figure of the first group is equipped in a quilted tunic or shirt, with long sleeves tightly fastened at the wrists; precisely similar in appearance to the quilted tunic of the West Highland effigies. He carries a long spear in his left hand and wears a skull-cap with circular ear-plates. The figure on his left is that of a man wearing a short-sleeved hauberk of mail with divided skirt, over a long tunic, which is represented without the ridged appearance suggestive of quilting. It has long sleeves fastened at the wrists. The hauberk is confined at the waist by a belt, and the neck and shoulders are covered by a vandyked gorget. His head is protected by a burgonet; in his left hand he carries a bow, with a sheaf of arrows under his arm. His right hand grasps the hilt of a great two-handed sword, borne over the right shoulder. Behind these are the three figures of the second group, representing the poorer class of fighting men. They are destitute of body-armour, and no two of them are armed or clad alike. The foremost wears a rough mantle thrown over the shoulders and partially covering the head, under the mantle the skirt of a long tunic or shirt is visible, and the feet are bare. He carries under the left arm a two-handed sword. The two behind him are both armed with pole-axes. One wears a sort of doublet over the long tunic or shirt; the other has no covering on the breast, his upper garment hanging loosely over the shoulders.

ARMS AND EQUIPMENT.

From the enactments passed by the Scottish Parliament for the regulation of the equipments of the different classes liable to be called on for military service, from the fourteenth century downwards, it appears that though there were great variations in the character of the arms and the general equipment of these classes at different periods, the use of body armour was always confined to the comparatively wealthy. The utmost term of service which the king was entitled to exact at one time was forty days, and all between the ages of sixteen and sixty were liable to be summoned for the defence of the country. They were bound to provide their own arms and armour; and in order to ensure that these should be conformable to the statutes, and kept in good order, weaponshaws were appointed to be held at stated periods.

In 1318 it was enacted that persons worth £10 in goods should have an acton and bassinet, or a habergeon and hat of iron, with gloves of iron, a spear and a sword; while those who were worth a cow were each to possess a good spear, or a good bow with a sheaf of twenty-four arrows. In 1448 persons coming to the host and worth £15 of land or 40 merks in goods were to have a horse, a hauberkion, a steel bonnet, a sword and a dagger; those worth between 40 and 100 shillings of land were each to possess a bow and arrows, a dagger and knife; such as were of less estate were to have gysarms (i.e. hand-axes), bow and arrows, and all others bows and arrows only. In the early part of the fifteenth century the scarcity of arms and armour in the country is indicated by the fact that merchants were enjoined to bring home from each voyage harness, armour, spear-shafts, and bow-staves, in proportion to their merchandise.

In the sixteenth century, when the use of fire-arms was becoming general, the landed men are enjoined to provide themselves with hagbuts of found and culverins; and every merchant was ordered to bring home two or more hagbuts each voyage, or metal to make them. In the weapon-schaws of 1535 halberts, cross-bows, and two-handed swords appear. In 1552 the Privy Council ordered a levy of two regiments of foot from Huntly's sheriffdom in the Highlands, to assist the King of France in his wars. They were to be armed "with jack and plait, steillbonett, swerd, buckler, new hois and doublett of canvouse at the lest; and slevis of plait or splenttis, and ane speir of sax elne lang or thereby." But this was not the distinctive equipment of the Highlanders; for in 1574, when a general order for weaponshawing was issued for the whole kingdom, we find that it contains a separate regulation for the Highlands. The general appointment is that all persons under 300 merks of yearly rent must have "brigantinis, jakkis, steilbonettis, slevis of plate or mail, swerds, pikkis, or speris of sex elnis lang, culverings, halbertis, or twa-handit swordis." But in the Highlands the equipment was to be "habirschonis, steilbonettis, hektonis, swordis, bowis and dorlochis,[*] or culveringis." **The records of the** Privy Council show the common weapons carried by the clans in their internecine **feuds. The** M'Kenzies of Kintail appear in an attack on the Bishop's house **at Chanonry in 1578,** "**bodin in** feir of weir with hagbuttis, bowis, swords." Maclean of Dowart's men **appear in** "habirschonis, armed with bowis and dorlochis;" and the men of Kintail attack Glengarry with "twa-handit-swordis, bowis, dorlochis, hagbuttis and pistolettis."

At the same period the Lowland men engaged in "tulzies," requiring the interference of **the executive, appear** "bodin with jakkis steilbonettis, pistolettis, speiris, **lang hagbuts and Jedburgh staffis.**" The watchmen of the burghs, as in Edinburgh, **were armed with** "**lang waippinis," and the** merchants and craftsmen having booths **or** dwelling houses in the foregait were **to be sufficiently** provided with such weapons as the "aichis (axe), halbartis, and Jedburgh staffis, for stopping **of** tuilye."[†] In Peebles, in 1369, the watchers went round the town nightly armed **with** jack and steel-bonnet, sword and buckler.[‡]

In 1598 the carrying of fire-arms, unless in the King's service, is prohibited. At this time Earls, Lords, and Barons are to be armed with corslet of proof, head-piece, vambraces, tessletis, and Spanish pike; gentlemen worth 300 marks of yearly rent were to have a corslet and pike, or musket and head-piece; and inhabitants of burghs worth £500 were to have corslet, pike, halbert, and two-handed sword, or else musket and head-piece. And "because there is na sic quantity of armour made within this realm," Sir Michael Balfour of Burley receives a monopoly of the sale for three years, and undertakes **to** import arms for two thousand horsemen and **eight** thousand foot. The prices fixed were:—

A horseman's armour complete, . .	£50	0	0
The same, but "proof of the hagbut," .	60	0	0
A footman's armour complete, .	18	0	0
A hagbut with flask and banderole, .	6	13	4

In the seventeenth century the equipment of the fighting men was exceedingly varied. The levy called out by the Convention of Estates in 1643 included all men between the ages of sixteen and sixty; the horsemen to be armed with pistols, broadswords, and steel caps; the footmen with musket and sword, or pike and sword, and when these could not be had, with "halberts, Lochwaber axes, or Jedburgh staffis and swords." In the middle of **this century, Gordon** of Rothiemay describes the arms of the Highlanders as follows:—"Their weapons are a bow, **and a quiver full of** bearded arrows, which hangs on their thigh, a poniard and **broadsword, and some of them have** two-handed-swords." But the most valuable sources of information regarding **the arms and** armour in use in the Highlands at this period are the inventories of the "plenissing" **of the great** Highland houses, of which, unfortunately, but few have yet been printed. The most **curious of** these are the inventories of the goods and gear in the houses of Balloch and Finlarig, belonging to Sir Duncan Campbell of Glenurchy and his son Sir Colin, and dated respectively **in** 1600 and 1640. Their special features are thus summarised by Cosmo Innes, **in his** preface **to** "The Black Book of Taymouth":—

"The Artillery was not formidable, though probably more than required in Highland warfare. The hand guns, muskets, hagbuts of snap-work or of rowet work, or of lent work, (matchlocks) prove the value in which they were held by the minuteness of the description of their ornaments, whether stocked with Brissel,

(Brazil wood), or inlaid with bone or with pearl, or gilt pieces with the Laird's arms. There is the usual array of arms from the primitive hand-bow and its bag of arrows to horsemen's harness with steel bonnets, plate gloves, corslets, murrions of proof, steel targes, and two-handed swords. There are Jedburgh staffs and Lochaber axes, but there is nothing of 'the ancient Highland broad-sword.' Andrew Ferrara's name is not found. The most curious, as well as the most careful and formal of these inventories is the one made up in 1640, when Sir Colin and his sons, a few months before his death, agreed to set aside certain articles as his heir-looms. The arms set apart are field pieces of copper and iron, and a few muskets and pistols, a pair of two-handed swords, one with its hilt overlaid with velvet, three targets, two of steel, and one of cork, and a quantity of body armour all of plate."

To this it may be added that the muskets and hagbuts are mostly described as inlaid or "indentit" with bone or mother-of-pearl. The pistols are sometimes mentioned as of brass, and there is evidence that some of the most highly ornamented muskets were manufactured in Scotland. For instance, in the inventory of the "graith" in charge of the porter of the House of Balloch in 1600, there is "ane lang hagbute that was maid in Dundie, gilt with the Lardis armis," and in the "compt of the gunnis quhilk the Larde lies in his awn handis" there is mention of another "gilt pece with the Lardis armis that come out of Dundie, stockit with brissell," and "ane uther schoirt quhyte pece that came out of Dundie, with the Lardis armis thairon," and a "hagbute that come out of Menteith." In an inventory of 1605 of the arms in charge of the porter at Balloch, we meet with the arms of which Sir Michael Balfour of Burley had the monopoly of sale (as previously noticed), together with horsemen's armour from Leith, and targets gilt with gold:—

> "Mair thair of muscattis that come fra the Larde of Burley, indentit with mother of perle with
>   lunt work, ii.
> "Item targis ourgilt with gold that come fra the Priorie of Charterhous, i.
> "Item, mair of steill targis, i.
> "Item horsemen standis of armour that come out of Leith, iii stand, .   iii"

It is curious to find that at this late date when muskets, hagbuts, and pistols were so common, the bow and arrows were still reckoned an ordinary part of the equipement of the Highland levies. In 1627, King Charles I. writes to his trusty and well-beloved the Laird of Glenurchy, informing him that warrant had been granted to Alexander M'Naughtan, for levying two hundred bowmen for service in the war with France:—"And being informed that the persons in those high countries are ordinarlie good bowmen we are hereby well-pleased to desire you to use your best means to cause levy such a nomber of them for our said servant as possiblie you can." Again in June 1633 the Chancellor, Kinnoul, writes to the Laird of Glenurchy, that the King is desirous that at the time of his coming to Perth there may be "a show and muster made of hielandmen, in their countrie habite and best order," and desires Glenurchy to select from his followers and dependents "men personable for stature and in their best array and equipage, with trews, bowes, dorloches, and others their ordinaire weapons and furniture," and send them to Perth on the 8th July following. In the muster roll of Glenurchy's men in 1638, among one hundred and seventeen men sixty-four were armed with sword and target, thirty-seven had bows and arrows, and thirty-one carried hagbuts. Sometimes the bow and arrows were carried with the sword and target, and sometimes the hagbut. At other times the bow and arrows were the sole equipment, and occasionally it is noted that the sword is the only weapon in the man's possession.

The anonymous writer of a description of "The Highland Host"* brought into the south-

---

* Wodrow MSS., Advocates' Library. Printed in "Blackwood's Edinburgh Magazine" for April 1817, p. 68.

western counties in 1678 to suppress the Presbyterian conventicles, refers to their "head pieces and steel-bonnets raised like pyramids, targets and shields of the most odde and antique forme, and powder-horns hung on strings and garnished with beaten-nails and burnished brass." "And truely," he adds, "I doubt not but a man curious in our antiquities, might in this host finde explications of the strange pieces of armour mentioned in our old lawes, such as basnet, iron hat, gorgets, pesane, wambrassers, and reerbrassers, panns, leg-splents, and the like, above what any occasion in the Lowlands would have afforded for several hundreds of years." Cleland, who wrote a satirical poem on the same expedition * hits off the salient characteristics of the Highland officers as follows:—

"But those who were their chief commanders	A bagg which they with onions fill
As such who bore the pirnie standards	And as their strick observers say
Who led the van and drove the rear	A tupe horn filled with usquebay ;
Were right well mounted of their geir ;	A slasht out coat beneath his plaides
With brogues, trues, and pirnie plaides	A targe of timber, nails and hides ;
With good blew bonnets on their heads	With a long two-handed sword
Which on the one side had a flipe	As goods the country can afford ;
Adorned with a tobacco-pipe,	Had they not need of bulk and bones
With duck and snap-work and snuff-mill	Who fight with all these arms at once."

Sacheverell in his descriptions of the Highlanders of Mull in 1688, alludes to the sporran, which he terms a large shot pouch, on each side of which hangs a pistol and a dagger, a round target on their backs, a blue bonnet on their heads, in one hand a broad sword and a musket in the other—perhaps no nation goes better armed.

After the Revolution of 1688 the importation of arms was chiefly from Holland. But there was no further change in the Highland equipment, which consisted of sword and target, pistols and dirk, with or without the addition of a musket, or a Lochaber axe. At Killiecrankie, the sword and target won the day, and it is recorded of this action that the delay consequent on unfixing the plug bayonet having been ascribed as one cause of the defeat of the English troops, a bayonet with rings to be fixed upon the barrel instead of being inserted in it was devised by General Mackay.

The Rebellion of 1715 was followed by a disarming Act which made it penal for any one to have in his custody or to use or wear "broadsword or target, poignard, whinger or dirk, side-pistol, gun or other warlike weapon." The muster roll of the Clan Ranald in 1745 shows that out of eighty men, sixteen had neither gun nor sword, sixteen had guns only, fifteen had swords only, twenty-five had gun and sword, and only seven were equipped with gun, sword, and target. The rigorous enforcement of the disarming Acts, first in 1716 and subsequently in 1725 and 1746, was fatal to the preservation of the proscribed arms. † The specimens that have been saved from the general destruction are therefore few in number, but they are rendered all the more interesting by their rarity. They have additional features of interest in the excellence of their workmanship and the beauty of their decoration. The classification and grouping of the examples selected by Mr Drummond facilitates comparison, and invites a few notices of the general characteristics and historical relations of the different classes.

* "Collection of Poems," &c., by William Cleland, Lieutenant-Colonel to the Earl of Angus's Regiment, 1697, p. 12.

† In 1716 the arms delivered up to the agents of the Government were paid for, and General Wade complains that nearly £13,000 was paid for broken and useless arms. In 1725 he complains that the people, knowing they were not to be paid for the arms they might surrender, carried them to the forges and turned them into working tools and other peaceable instruments. Nevertheless the number of arms collected this year in the Highlands, of the several species mentioned in the Disarming Act, amounted in the whole to 2685, the greater part of which were deposited in the Castle of Edinburgh.— "General Wade's Report concerning the Highlands in 1725."

HIGHLAND TARGETS.

The form of the Highland Target is round, usually from 19 to 21 inches diameter. It is constructed of two layers of some light wood, often of fir, the grain of the one layer crossing that of the other angularly, and the pieces dowelled together. Over the wood, a covering of leather is tightly stretched for the front of the target, and a piece of hide, often of calf-skin, with a stuffing for the back. A handle, sometimes of leather (as in Plate IV. Fig. 6), sometimes of iron (as in Plate IV. Fig. 5), and an arm-strap (as shown in both these figures) were fixed at the back, near the opposite sides of the circumference of the target. Occasionally there were two arm-straps (as in Plate I. Fig. 2), and sometimes instead of arm-straps, a sleeve of leather was fastened to the back of the target (as seen in Plate V. Fig. 4). A boss of brass usually occupies the centre of the front of the target. The boss was occasionally pierced for a spike which screwed into a socket at the base of the boss. The spike is shown in position in the Ardvoirlich target (in Plate V.), and the socket into which it was screwed is visible in one of the targets in the National Museum (shown as Fig. 5 of Plate V.), in which the boss is wanting. When not in use the spike was carried in a sheath at the back of the target (as shown in Plate I. Fig. 6).

The ornamentation of these targets is peculiar and highly effective. The central boss is frequently surrounded by other bosses placed in the centres of contiguous circles defined by rows of nail-heads. The spaces between the circles are decorated by studs, or by segmental plates of brass, fastened with studs in the centre, and with nails round the borders, and ornamented with pierced or engraved work. These plates, when of pierced work, were placed over a lining of scarlet cloth, which showed through the openings (as in Plate I. Fig. 5, and Plate V. Fig. 5). Sometimes the bosses themselves were thus pierced and lined (as in Plate IV. Fig 3). Occasionally the decoration is confined to the formation of simple geometric patterns, on the face of the target, by the disposition of the studs and nail-heads (as in Plate IV. Fig. 1., and Plate VII. Fig. 4). Sometimes this simple form of decoration is conjoined with the use of nails and studs (as in Plate VII. Fig. 3). But more frequently the surface of the leather covering is tooled with a variety of patterns, disposed in symmetrical spaces. The style of this ornament corresponds to that engraved on the Powder Horns and Brooches; and the designs in general have a close affinity with those of the later stone and metal work of the Celtic school of art, as exemplified in the West Highland Crosses, the Crosier of St Fillan, and the Bell-shrine of Kirkmichael Glassary. On the leather-work of the targets animal forms are rare. The prevailing ornaments are foliageous scroll-work and interlacing patterns. In two cases (Plate I. Figs. 3 and 5), they exhibit what seem to be armorial bearings, though not treated according to the rules of heraldry; and in two cases (Plate V. Figs. 1 and 2) they present initials and dates—both subsequent to the disarming Act of 1716. Judging from a comparison of the style of the two that are dated, with that of the undated specimens, there can be little doubt that the purer style, seen in the Ardvoirlich target for instance (Plate V. Fig. 3), is very much earlier. But the absence of dated characteristics for the styles of Celtic ornament prevents a close approximation to the periods of its different varieties, and a much wider knowledge of its various manifestations is required for the determination of local peculiarities and chronological sequences.

The earliest known specimens of Scottish shields are represented in Plate VII. Figs. 1 and 2.

If the wooden object (Fig. 1) be really a shield, as Mr Drummond believed it to be, its period is quite uncertain. But that represented in Fig. 2 is one of a class of bronze shields of which four examples have been found in Scotland. They are formed of thin beaten bronze, and ornamented with concentric rings and circles of studs, placed alternately and close together so as to cover the whole surface. The rings and studs are in *repoussé* work, and the border of the shield is a wider ring beaten out and turned over to the inside. These shields are attributed to the close of the bronze age, that is, to a period preceding the conquest of Southern Britain by the Romans. They differ from the Highland targets in having only a simple handle placed under the central boss. The round target with a central boss, sometimes with bosses disposed round it, as in several of the Highland examples, appears not unfrequently on the sculptured monuments both of Eastern and Western Scotland, as for example on a fragment of a sculptured stone from Dull, now in the National Museum, on the shaft of the Dupplin Cross, on the monument at Benvie, and on a sepulchral slab at Kilmory. Most of the recumbent effigies of the West Highlands, however, present the heater-shaped shield, charged with a heraldic cognizance.

The use of the target in Scotland was not confined to the Highlands. The statutory equipment appointed by the Act of 1425, for such yeomen or burgesses as were not archers, was "sword and buckler, and a good axe or broggit staff;" and in 1481 the axemen who had neither spear nor bow were required to provide themselves with targes "of tree" or leather, according to patterns which were sent to each of the sheriffs. The watchers of the burgh of Peebles, in 1569, were armed with jack and spear, sword and buckler. In an account of Queen Mary's journey to Inverness in 1562, the English Ambassador, Randolph, writing to Cecil [*] describes her cheerful behaviour in the midst of troubles, and says that "she repented nothing but (when the lords and others at Inverness came in the morning from the watch) that she was not a man to know what life it was to lie all night in the fields, or to walk on the causeway with a jack and knapschalle, a Glasgow buckler and a broadsword." It may be inferred from this incidental expression that such bucklers as were then used at Inverness, by the "lords and others," were manufactured in Glasgow. But the probability is, that the manufacture of the Highland targets, as we now know them, was not confined to any particular locality. That they were made in large numbers, on short notice, in 1745, is shown by the following entries in the accounts of Laurence Oliphant of Gask,[†] as paymaster for Prince Charles at Perth :—

1745		
Nov. 15. To Wm. Lindsay, wright, for six score targets,	£30 14 6	
1746		
Jan. 16. To Wm. Lindsay for 247 targets—		
To 24 Hyds leather from the tannage,	£16 16	
To Goat skins, wood, nails, &c.,	15 10	
To two Officers targets pr. order,	1	
Feb. 3. To Wm. Lindsay for paying leather of 200 targes,	16 16	

It appears from this that the cost of two officer's targets, made to order, was but 10s. each, and the cost of the others about 5s. each.

It appears also that targets were made in Edinburgh in 1745. In the orders for the Highland Army of 10th and 11th October 1745, given at Holyrood House, Colonel Lord Ogilvy orders that

* = Calendar of State Papers, Foreign," 1562. P. 304.
† "Jacobite Lairds of Gask." By T. L. Kington Oliphant. Grampian Club, pp. 136, 166.

E

all the officers of his regiment shall "provide themselves in targes from the armourers in Edinburgh."[*] These, however, were probably made to order like those at Perth. The older targets fared badly after the Disarming Acts. Boswell, describing the weapons in Dunvegan Castle in 1773, says there is hardly a target now to be found in the Highlands; after the Disarming Acts they made them serve as covers to their buttermilk barrels. In the case of two of the finest of those figured by Mr Drummond only the ornamented leather remained. Another of the finer specimens was rescued from a coal-cellar in 1870.

Targets were carried by some of the men of the Black Watch when first embodied in 1740, and Grose mentions that he remembered "many private men of the old Highland Regiment in Flanders, in the years 1747 and 1748, armed with targets which, though no part of their uniform, they were permitted to carry."

SWORDS.

The Highland Broadsword (as has been previously remarked) does not appear in the inventories of the arms of such Highland houses as Balloch and Finlarig in the beginning of the seventeenth century. It is a special variety of a type of weapon which came into use as a cavalry sword towards the end of that century. Basket-hilted swords, in which the basket is more oval in form than in the Highland variety, were carried by the *schiavoni*, or guards of the Doges of Venice, in the early part of the seventeenth century. Specimens of this Venetian type of weapon are given in Plate VIII. Figs. 6 and 7, and Plate IX. Figs. 7 and 8. Specimens of basket-hilted cavalry swords, assigned to the latter part of the seventeenth century, are preserved in the Musée d'Artillerie at Paris. The broadsword first appears in formal record in Scotland in 1643, when, along with the Lochaber axe and the Jedburgh staff, it constitutes part of the equipment of the levies then called out by the Convention of Estates. From 1582 to 1649 a "ribbit gaird" often appears as the "essay" of the armourers of Edinburgh, but in 1649 it was changed to "ane mounted sword, with a new scabbard and an Highland guard."[†] Many of the Scottish basket-hilted swords have Ferara blades, but this does not necessarily imply that they are older than the period indicated. A basket-hilted sword 3 feet 5½ inches in length, including the hilt, bearing on each side of the blade a medallion portrait, and inscribed "General Oliver Cromwell," with several mottoes in Latin, is preserved in the Dover Museum. But the earliest, and indeed the only dated specimen of the Scottish basket-hilted sword, which persistent search has produced is a fine specimen of the variety of which Nos. 3 and 4 of Plate X. are examples. It is almost exactly of the form of No. 3, but the hilt, which is of silver, is of finer make and more highly ornamented. It bears the letters C.R. under a crown as the centre ornament of the basket, and on the broad rib of the basket, next the royal monogram, is engraved the following inscription :—

"Att Huntly Castle, the second Fryday of Sept' 1701. Worne at King Charles the 2ᵈ fare. All horses not exceiding ane 100 merks pryce were admitted the ryders stalking crouns which was given to the poore who were obligged to pray that the Monarchie and Royall famelie may be lasting and glorious in this kingdoms. Worne be Ja: Drummond in Drimmaquhance."

[*] March of the Highland Army in the Years 1745-46. By Captain James Stuart of Lord Ogilvy's Regiment. "Spalding Club Miscellany." Vol. I. p. 278.

[†] Observations on the Hammermen of Edinburgh.—"Archæologia Scotica." Vol. I p. 173.

On the rib below the inscription there are two stamps, one a monogram V S and the other ELGIN. Round the pommel is another inscription :—

"Taken at Dunblain by one of Evan's Dragoons."

This sword was exhibited by the Duchess of Gordon at the Exhibition of Works of Art, &c., held at Aberdeen on the occasion of the meeting of the British Association there in 1859.* The first inscription shows that it was made at Elgin as a prize to be run for at a horse race at King Charles the Second's Fair at Huntly. This explains the presence of the royal monogram and the crown, which would have borne a different interpretation if the second inscription only had survived.

In Plates VIII. and IX. there are several examples of the famed Ferara blades which, for some unknown reason, attained exceptional popularity in Scotland. Nothing is certainly known of the swordsmith originally using the designation of Andrea Ferara, beyond the excellence of the blades that bear his mark by right. He is said to have been an Italian armourer of the last quarter of the sixteenth century, and to have also established an armoury in Spain. But this is probably a mere inference, from the fact that the cognomen of the artificer is by some supposed to have been derived from the town of Ferrara in Italy, and by others from the town of Feraria in the north of Spain. It may be of some significance that the name of Ferreira is still common in Spain, and that, while Farara sword-blades are almost unknown in Italy, the largest and finest collection of them in existence is to be found in the Royal Arsenal at Madrid.† The name "Andrea Ferara em Lisboa" occurs on a sword in the possession of Brodie of Brodie ;‡ and there is a sword stamped with the words "O. Cromwell L. Prokter," which also bears the armourer's mark "Andrea Ferara," and the name of the German town Solingen.§ The date usually attributed to the original Andrea is too early for the majority of the sword-blades bearing the designation, and the probability is, that the "Farara" blade was manufactured by various armourers in different places to supply the demand created, in the first instance, by their superior excellence. Piero Ferara, Cosmo Ferara, and Giovanni Fuerara, are signatures occasionally found on sword-blades, and it is quite in accordance with what is known, in other cases, that the original name Andrea should have been continued through several generations of armourers after it had once become famous.

The great two-handed swords of the sixteenth and seventeenth centuries, also appear to have been popular in the Highlands. Gordon of Rothiemay refers to them in the middle of the seventeenth century, as still used by some of the Highlanders of Aberdeenshire, while others used the broadsword. The pictures of the Campbells of Glenurchy in the "Black Book of Taymouth," drawn about the end of the sixteenth or beginning of the seventeenth century, represent them and their followers with two-handed swords. In the inventory of the "geir" left by Sir Colin Campbell at Balloch and Finlarig in 1640, there is :—

"Ane two-handit sword, the hand quhairof is overlayed with velvet.
"Ane uther two-handit sword with ane loose hand to be eikit thairto."

---

* Mr Drummond does not seem to have known of this sword, which would have been possessed of an intense interest for him.

† It appears from the Ledger of Andrew Halyburton that Spanish swords were occasionally imported into Scotland as early as 1493.

‡ Cited in a paper on "Andrea Ferara Swords," by G. V. Irving, in which a series of rubbings of the marks and signatures of twenty-five Scottish specimens, by Mr J. D. Greenshields, are described. Mr Irving very properly refers to the legend of Andrea Ferara being brought to Scotland by James IV. or V., and working in the Highlands, tempering blades in a dark cellar, and killing his son for attempting to steal his secret, as a myth.—"Archæological Association's Journal," Vol. XXI, p. 316.

§ "Catalogue of the Exhibition of Industrial Art at Alcoats, 1883." By W. Wareing Faulder. Page 6.

and in another inventory of 1605 there is a two-handed sword specified as "gilt with gold." The swords represented in the pictures of the "Black Book" were probably drawn from the originals in the armoury at the time. They all have straight guards except the two which the artist has placed in the hands of the first Colin of Glenurchy and the first Earl of Argyle, which have the guards curved towards the point. The two-handed sword first appears in the weapon-shaws of the first-half of the sixteenth century. The series of these weapons shown in Plates XI.-XIII. illustrates the varieties now met with in Scotland, which are for the most part similar to those of the continent.

But the variety with the reversed guard, having the quillons bent angularly towards the point of the weapon (as shown in the specimens on Plate XV.) is interesting because it so closely resembles the sword carved on the West Highland monuments, and because it occurs more frequently in Scotland than anywhere else. * A fine example of this form of sword, having the quillons of the guard bent angularly towards the point, and terminating in pierced quatrefoils, was destroyed in the fire at Warwick Castle. One in the possession of the late Keith Stewart Mackenzie of Seaforth, has the blade marked with an orb and cross—a common Spanish mark of the sixteenth century. But none of them exhibit the peculiar character of the pommel and guard which is distinctive of the sword most frequently carved on the monuments, as shown in the swords of the two effigies figured on page 9. The triangular multi-lobed pommel so constantly seen in these effigies is an earlier form of which no actual specimen is known to exist in Scotland. It was a common form of the pommel of the Norse sword of the close of the Viking period—that is, in the last half of the eleventh and beginning of the twelfth centuries.† In the Norse swords this multi-lobed pommel was associated with the curved guard, shown in Figs. 2 and 8 of Plate XIV. In the West Highland effigies, some of which must be as late as the fifteenth century, it is usually associated with the angularly reversed guard. A singled-handed sword of early date with a wheel-shaped pommel and a guard of this form, which is preserved in the National Museum, is shown as Fig. 1 of Plate XVI. These swords, and not the basket-hilted broadswords, are the true Highland swords to which the poetical name of *claymore* may be fitly applied.

HIGHLAND DIRKS.

The Highland Dirk is distinguished from all other weapons of the same kind by its long triangular blade single-edged and thick-backed; and by its peculiar handle, cylindrical, without a guard, but shouldered at the junction with the blade, the grip swelling in the middle, and the pommel circular and flat-topped. Its most characteristic feature is the carving of the handle, which is invariably in one style of knot-work, the different specimens exhibiting considerable variety of treatment. Occasionally the hilts are entirely of brass. One of these brass-hilted dirks bears the date 1693.

The earliest of the dirks figured in Plates XVII-XIX. is perhaps the short-bladed plain-handled specimen, Fig. 4 of Plate XVII., which was found with a knife-blade of iron in a grave at

---

* The specimen No. 7 (Plate XV.), bearing an inscription on the blade, is probably English. It belonged to the hermit of Barnard Castle, Durham, who stated that he obtained it at the dispersion of the effects of Miss Lees of Scalindrop Hall. It is now at Alnwick Castle.

† One of these Norse swords, with a Runic inscription—"Asmund made me, Aslak owns me,"—and a foliageous scroll engraved on the grip, is figured by Professor Stephens in the "Old Northern Runic Monuments of Scandinavia and England," Vol. III. p. 168.

East Langton, Mid-Lothian. There are two of exceptional form, viz.—No. 7 of Plate XVII. which is in the collection of Mr Gourlay Steell, and is said to have been found at Prestonpans, and No. 8 of Plate XIX., which its possessor, Sir J. Noel Paton, regards as of Athole manufacture. Both differ from the ordinary dirk in the form of the blade and in the peculiarity of having a rudimentary guard. The sheath of the dirk was often made of stamped leather, sometimes finely ornamented with interlacing patterns in keeping with the ornamentation of the handle. The fashion of carrying a knife and fork in the side sheaths is at least as old as the time of Charles I. Mr Boutell instances "a beautiful dagger, now the property of Mr Kerslake, that appears to have been worn by King Charles I. when he was Prince of Wales; the hilt has the plume of three ostrich feathers, and a knife and fork are inserted in the sheath."

The earliest mention of the dirk as a customary part of the Highland equipment, occurs in John Major's notice of the dress and armour of the Highlanders, written in 1512, in which he says that they carry a large dagger, sharpened on one side only, but very sharp, under the belt. In the previous century Blind Harry refers to the custom of carrying a Scots Whittle under the belt. Describing the meeting of Wallace with the son of the English Constable of Dundee, he makes the Englishman address him thus :—

> " He callyt on him and said Thou Scot abyde
> Quha dewill the grathis in so gay a gyde
> Ane Ersche mantill it war the kynd to wer
> A Scottis thewtill undyr the belt to ber
> Rouch rewlyngis upon the harlot fete."

General Wade mentions the custom of swearing on the dirk, which came to his notice among the Clan Cameron and others who followed their example in putting down the practice of taking *Tascall* money, or a reward given in secret for information regarding stolen cattle. "To put a stop to this practice which they thought an injury to the tribe, the whole clan of the Camerons (and others since by their example) bound themselves by oath never to take *Tascall* money. This oath they take upon a drawn dagger, which they kiss in a solemn manner, and the penalty declared to be due to the breach of the said oath is to be stabbed with the same dagger ; this manner of swearing is much in practice on all other occasions to bind themselves to one another."

POWDER **HORNS**.

The Highland Powder Horn is also distinguished from all others by its peculiarities of form and ornament. It is made from a neat's horn, flattened, and fitted with a wooden bottom, and a plug for the mouth, which is frequently also encircled with a mounting of lead. The manner in which it was carried is seen in the engraving on the powder horn assigned to Sir George Mackenzie of Tarbat, previously referred to, in the remarks on the Highland Dress. No portion of the Highlander's equipment appears to have been more prized or more beautifully decorated, and no example of the beauty and grace of the prevailing style of decoration is more effective than that of King Charles's "Master of the Game," figured in Plate XX. The oldest specimen bearing a date is No. 5 of Plate XXIII., belonging to Sir J. Noel Paton, R.S.A., which is inscribed with the initials J D. 1643. The finest in decoration after the one bearing the monogram of Sir George Mackenzie, are No. 5 of Plate XXII., dated 1678; No. 3 of the same Plate, dated 1685; No. 1 of Plate XXIII., dated 1691 ; and No. II. of Plate XXV., dated 1672. The estimation in which these

highly decorated objects of home manufacture,—the designing and engraving of which was wholly
of individual effort,—may be inferred from the mottoes they bear, if not from the careful work and
original character of the designs. One commemorates a friendly gift (No. 2, Plate XXIII.);
another, No. 1 of Plate XXV., records the owner's declaration :—

> " I love the As my Wyffe
> I'll keip the As my Lyffe,"

and adds the sententious motto :—

> " A man his mynd should never sets
> W'pon A thing he can not gett."

HIGHLAND PISTOLS.

The Highland Pistol exhibits three varieties of form, with the globose, the lobed, and the ram's
horn butt. They are wholly formed of metal, usually of steel, sometimes of brass, and occasionally
in part of both these metals. Like most other portions of the Highland equipment they are always
remarkable for the excellence of their manufacture and the beauty of their decoration. Probably
the earliest of those figured in the Plates XXVI.-XXVIII. is No. 5 of Plate XXVIII. which is
not, however, distinctly Highland in character. Mr Drummond possessed a steel pistol with
engraved brass stock dated 1645. The short rifled pistol, No. 4 of Plate XXVIII., the property of
Mr Gourlay Steell, R.S.A., is dated 1665. The beautiful example figured as No. 1 of Plate XXVII.
is dated 1700. Mr Glen has a wheel-lock pistol of the time of Charles I. on which the armourer's
mark is a pair of bagpipes and the initials C. L. Logan states that the manufacture of pistols was
commenced at Doune about 1646 by Thomas Caddell who had learned his trade at Muthil. One of
his apprentices, John Campbell, also became a famous maker. John Murdoch succeeded him.
Campbell's and Murdoch's pistols are more common than Caddell's. Bissett occurs frequently on
Highland pistols in the Tower Armoury. A less known maker is Jo. Chrystie. A brace of his
pistols are in the collection of Sir J. Noel Paton, R.S.A. They have ram's horn butts, and are of
such extraordinary beauty of design, delicacy of workmanship, and perfection of condition, that
Sir Noel says of them in his "Private Catalogue" (so often quoted in the pages of this work), "I
have nowhere seen pistols more, or indeed so, beautiful as these." Another maker whose work is
not widely known is Alexander Shireff, or Shiress, Old Meldrum.

In 1650 the horseman's equipment consisted of pistols, lance, broadsword, and steel cap, and
the price of a pair of pistols with holster and spanner was fixed at £14. The price of a pair of
Doune pistols, according to Logan, varied from four to twenty-four guineas.

MUSKETS.

The Muskets though exhibiting less of the peculiar decoration of the dirk, the powder-horn,
and the pistol, are nevertheless distinguished by their ornate character. They are fewer in number
because they were more costly weapons, and their use was confined to the comparatively wealthy.
Reference has already been made to the fact that the inventories of the Houses of Balloch and
Finlarig show that they were made in Dundee, and that their ornamentation consisted of engraved
work and inlaid work in bone and mother-of-pearl. The details of the ornamentation of the three

specimens figured on Plate XXX. will show how rich and beautiful the decoration occasionally was. The inscription on the barrel of one of these (No. 3), which is also figured full length as No. 3 of Plate XXIX., shows that it was made in Germany to the order of John Grant, Sheriff of Inverness, but the date, 1434, is much too early for the piece as it now exists.

AXES.

The Axe is one of the earliest of weapons. The war-axe of iron, in its earlier forms, differed in no respect from the same implement used as a tool. The earliest form of the weapon-tool is shown on Plate XXXIV. as a common axe-head longer and narrower in the shank than those now in use. Such axes are depicted as weapons in the Bayeux tapestry. War-axes of a later time were furnished with prolongations in the line of the shaft and hammers or spikes on the back of the blade. The Jedburgh Staff was a long-handled axe with a curved or crescentic blade, with or without a back-spike. The Lochaber Axe had an elongated blade usually rounded at the upper end, and the staff was furnished with a hook on the end. Its different varieties are shown on Plates XXXII. and XXXIII. The glaives with hand-guards, figured on Plate XXXI., are of exceptional occurrence, and may be a Scottish variety. The axe and "broggit staff" appear in 1425 as the equipment of those who were not archers. In the weaponshaws of 1535 halberts appear along with two-handed swords. The Lochaber Axe and the Jeddard Staff appear in 1643 in company with the broadsword. In 1647 it was appointed that seventy-two men in each regiment should carry halbards, and in 1650 Lord Lorne requests a supply of partisans, from the store at Aberdeen, for the equipment of his regiment of Life Guards.

SPORRANS AND POUCHES.

The belt-pouches of the earlier form were simple bags ornamented with tags of leather. The Highland variety is distinguished by its ornamental clasp of metal, usually of brass, often engraved with foliageous scrolls and other devices, sometimes of pierced work inlaid like the ornamental pierced work of the target with scarlet cloth. The earlier form of these belt-pouches is shown in Plate XXXIX., and the distinctively Highland varieties in Plates XXXVI.-XXXVIII.

The small purse or *bursaid* in the gipsire form of general use in the later Middle Ages was worn by the Highlanders till 1746. In a portrait of George, second Earl of Seaforth, who died in 1651, the purse is of green cloth embroidered with gold and mounted with a gilt check-top fretted with silver. An example of the same kind in blue velvet embroidered with gold is in the posses-sion of Sir P. Murray Thriepland of Fingask. * The "bag which they with onions fill," which is noticed in the satirical description by Clelland, was the "maileid" or hunting bag, similar to those still used in various parts of the continent. Among the gentlemen, like the hawking-pouch of the sixteenth century, it was often of green cloth, or even velvet embroidered or "passmented" and ornamented with tassels. For the common men it was made of canvass or leather, and used for carrying their provisions in the chase or on a march; it differed in no respect from the haversack worn by the feudal retainers of the Middle Ages, and the regular troops of the present day. The

* "Costume of the Clans," by J. Sobieski and Charles Stuart, p. 83.

purse worn by Prince Charles Edward with his ordinary dress when on foot was of buckskin, embroidered with gold and closed with a silver check-top. When marching at the head of his army and completely armed with broadsword and target, dirk and pistols, he wore a purse of velvet embroidered with gold and silver, hung with gold cords and tassels and mounted with a gilt check-top, the semicircle of which was filled with the Royal Arms and supporters richly chased, and circumscribed below by a line of silver fringe.

BROOCHES.

The earlier form of the Celtic Brooch was penannular, with a long pin loosely looped on the body of the brooch, as shown in the examples figured at the bottom of Plate XLIV. The common Highland Brooch is annular in form, consisting of a broad flat circular body with a pin of the length of the diameter of the brooch. The head of the pin is usually split, and a portion of the body of the brooch is cut away to allow of its play upon a pivot which forms the junction of the two ends of the ring. In the older brooches the pin is quadrangular in section, the more modern form is round and tapering. The larger brooches are usually of brass. They are elaborately ornamented with circles filled with interlaced work, placed at regular intervals, the spaces between being filled with engraved patterns of a foliageous character, occasionally intermingled with figures of animals. A smaller variety of brooch in silver is ornamented with engraved work and patterns of peculiar form in niello. One of these is shown in Plate XLIV. Fig. 1. Only three varieties of these silver brooches, with patterns in niello, are known. Many of them bear initials and dates on the back, and all the dates are of the early part of the eighteenth century. They are sometimes termed Glasgow Brooches, from a supposition that they were all made in Glasgow, but it is asserted that one variety of them is known to have been made by a travelling tinker of the name of Ross, who frequented the country round Killin.

The heart-shaped brooches of silver, shown on Plate XLV., are known as Luckenbooth Brooches, from their having been commonly sold in the Luckenbooths, in the High Street of Edinburgh. They were "engaged" or betrothal presents. Many have such appropriate mottoes as :—

"Of earthly joys
Thou art my choice."

The heart which forms the body of the brooch was sometimes crossed by an A for Amor. One has the peculiar inscription "Ruth I. and 16th," and the date 1736. They frequently bore the initials of the parties with the dates on the back.

The great brooch of Ballochyle, Plate XLVI., is peculiar. It derives its interest chiefly from the setting in the centre, which gave it the character of a charm. These rock-crystal balls were regarded with veneration in the Middle Ages, and believed to be of peculiar potency and virtue. One was preserved in the house of Balloch, and is described in the inventory of 1640 as "ane stone of the quantitye of half a hen's egg, set in silver, being flatt at the ane end, and round at the uther end lyke ane peir, whilk Sir Coline Campbell first laird of Glenurchy woir when he fought in battell at the Rhodes against the Turks, he being one of the Knychtis of the Rhodes."

The Clach Dearg of Ardvoirlich, figured in the same Plate, is another instance. One mounted like the Ardvoirlich specimen belongs to the family of Baird of Auchmedden. Another similarly mounted, but with two rings opposite each other, belonged to the Campbells of Troup and Glenlyon.

MUSICAL INSTRUMENTS.

The harp and the bagpipes were the commonest of the musical instruments in use in Scotland, from the earliest times of which we have record. The harp, however, appears long before there is any mention of the bagpipe, as the favourite musical instrument of the Highlands. Representations of it occur on such sculptured monuments of the early Celtic period as those at Nigg, and Aldbar, and on the cross-shafts at Dupplin and Monifieth. A recumbent slab at Kiels in Knapdale, apparently of fourteenth or fifteenth century date, judging from the style of its ornament and the form of the sword sculptured on it, shows also the figure of a harp precisely similar in form and ornament to the "Queen Mary" Harp, Plate XLVIII. This remarkable instrument, now the property of John Steuart, Esq. of Dalguise, has been preserved in the family of the Robertsons of Lude from an early period; but its traditional history being obscure and unauthenticated by documentary evidence, it is impossible to assign to it a closely approximate date.* In the style of its ornamentation it approaches the West Highland Crosses and Slabs, which present the finest work. The beauty and grace of its decoration is unequalled by any known specimen of Scottish wood-work. The details of the ornament are shown in Plate XLIX. The Irish harp, preserved in Trinity College, Dublin, and popularly but erroneously attributed to the time of Brian Boru, is almost of the same form and somewhat similarly decorated, but in an inferior style. The Lamont Harp (Plate L.), also long in the family of the Robertsons of Lude, is a plainer instrument, but more massive in construction. It has no carved work, and its decoration is almost entirely confined to the engraved patterns of its mountings of brass. The harp figured in Plate LI. is an Irish specimen in the National Museum of Antiquities, Edinburgh, and considerably later in date than the Scottish examples.

The harp continued in use in the Highlands until about the commencement of the last century. Murdoch Macdonald, harper to Maclean of Coll, who died about 1740, was the last representative of the class of family musicians filling the once common hereditary office of harper to the chief of a clan. From the fifteenth to the eighteenth century, notices of wandering harpers are not uncommon. In the Accounts of the Lord High Treasurer of Scotland, harpers or "clareschawes" occur frequently as recipients of the royal bounty, especially at Pasch and Yule. Martyn M'Bretne, "Clareschawe," and another "Ersche," or Highland harper, are frequently mentioned, and a harper with one hand appears to have been among the musicians of James IV. Rewards given to harpers that were apparently not attached to the royal household, are also noted at Perth, Dumbarton, and Stirling.

The bagpipe is not peculiar to the Highlands of Scotland. It is an instrument which in various forms has been more or less common in many parts of Europe and Asia. But the Highland bagpipe is a variety of the instrument distinguished from all others by its peculiar characteristics. The special form of the modern instrument is not of great antiquity. Previous to the beginning of last century the Scottish bagpipe had no large or bass drone, and the Highland, Lowland, and Northumbrian bagpipes, were essentially the same instrument, though differing in external appearance, and in the method of inflation. Early specimens, however, are exceedingly

* A full examination of the traditionary history of the Lude Harps, by Charles D. Bell, with accurate descriptions and illustrations, is given in the "Proceedings of the Society of Antiquaries of Scotland," Vol. XV. pp. 10-33.

G

rare. The earliest and most interesting example of the Highland bagpipe now existing, is that shown in Plate XLVII., the property of Mr Robert Glen. It has but two drones and a chanter, and is finely ornamented with interlaced work and floral scrolls. It belongs to the early part of the fifteenth century, and bears the representation of a galley, the initials R. M'D., and the date 1409, carved on the stock in the characteristic style of the period. The piper survived the harper as the hereditary musician attached to the retinue of the chiefs of the clans. Most of the Scottish burghs also kept a piper to play through the streets at certain specified hours of the morning and evening. Both Chaucer and Shakespeare allude to the bagpipe as a common and familiarly known instrument in England, and occasional payments, by the Lord High Treasurer, to English pipers for playing before James IV., show that "the bagpipe was then at least as much identified with England as with Scotland." * But, "if the Gael cannot claim the merit of inventing the bagpipe, he can at least boast that he has made it his own, by inventing a style of execution which has turned the imperfections of the instrument into beauties, and has composed a rich and varied stock of music specially adapted for it, which cannot be properly performed on any other instrument." †

The series of drawings closes with a selection of wooden drinking vessels and agricultural and domestic implements. The drinking vessels, called methers, from their supposed use in drinking mead or metheglin, are more common in Ireland than in Scotland. They vary in height from 6 to 12 inches, having a capacity of from one to three pints, and the body of the vessel and its handles were always cut out of a single piece and the bottom inserted in a groove. They are rarely ornamented,—the only decorated example known in Scotland being a silver-mounted mether preserved at Dunvegan Castle.

The agricultural and domestic implements call for no special remark. But the presence of these objects in such a collection is an illustration of the fact that the rudeness of the implements used for common purposes in any condition of life is not necessarily an indication of the absence of those qualities of intellect and imagination whose exercise implies taste and produces culture. Had Mr Drummond lived to continue his collection until it became completely representative, while it would doubtless have illustrated more fully the peculiar phases of art and industry which give distinctive character and individuality to the story of the old Scottish life, it could scarcely have taught its most pregnant lesson with more powerful effect.

* " Accounts of the Lord High Treasurer of Scotland," edited by Thos. Dickson, p. cclv.
† Notes on the Ancient Musical Instruments of Scotland, by Robert Glen.—" Proceedings of the Society of Antiquaries of Scotland," Vol XIV., p. 123.

LIST OF PLATES.

PLATES.

PLATE I.—TARGETS

HIGHLAND TARGET of wood and leather, with boss of brass, engraved with an 1
arcaded pattern of semi-circles. The boss is surrounded by a circle of nail heads
close to its margin, and by a larger circle at a little distance from it. Round this circle
six similar but smaller circles are arranged symmetrically, and between them are
radiating rows of larger nail heads, and segmental plates of thin brass. The surface
of the leather within the circles is tooled in patterns of rosettes. This Target is in
the collection of Charles Tennant, Esq., of The Glen, Peeblesshire.

BACK OF TARGET, showing its lining of deer-skin fastened down with straps, and also the 2
arrangement of the handle and arm-straps of hide.

HIGHLAND TARGET of wood and leather, 20 inches diameter. The surface is divided into 3
a central circle, with two circular spaces surrounding it, each sub-divided into quadrants.
The leather is tooled so as to produce slightly raised patterns of scroll-work, partly of
foliageous, and partly of interlaced character. The patterns are repeated in each quadrant.
In the central circle is the figure of a double-headed eagle displayed. The divisions
of the surface and the edge of the Target are studded with nail heads, and the centre
is occupied by a stud instead of a boss. Bequeathed by the late Mr James Drummond,
R.S.A., to the National Museum of Antiquities, Edinburgh.

TARGET of iron on a framework of wood, the iron covering having a series of pyramidal 4
studs struck upon its surface, and a circle of conical bosses rivetted on, surrounding the
large central boss. It seems of Continental manufacture, probably German, and is in
the collection of Mr Charles Lees, R.S.A.

(a.) The same in profile.

HIGHLAND TARGET of wood and leather, 20 inches in diameter, the surface tooled, so as 5
to produce a slightly raised pattern of scroll-work of foliageous character, repeated
symmetrically round the boss, which rises from the centre of a quatrefoil of pierced
brass implanted on scarlet cloth, and surrounded by a circle of nail heads. Four smaller
bosses on similar quatrefoils are placed symmetrically round it, and alternately with them
a rosette with central stud. On the upper part of the Target is a galley, and beside it the
figure of a lion-like animal. The original is darker in colour than Mr Drummond's
drawing. This beautiful Target is in the collection of Sir J. Noel Paton, Kt., R.S.A.,
&c., who alludes to it in his "Private Catalogue of Armour, Weapons, &c." (1879) as
"rendered more than usually interesting by bearing on its surface three of the heraldic
achievements of Macdonald of Keppoch—the lion rampant, the lymphad, and the fish."

BACK OF A TARGET, showing its lining of deer-skin, handle, and arm-strap, and sheath for 6
the spike 10 inches long, which was fastened into the boss, by a screw, the thread
of which is visible protruding from the sheath. This Target is preserved at Ardvoirlich
House, Perthshire.

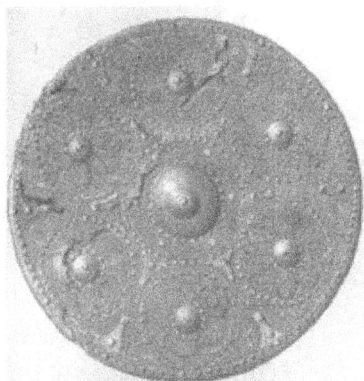

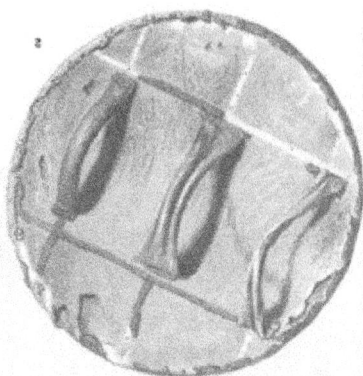

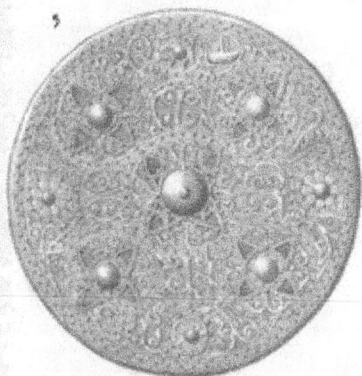

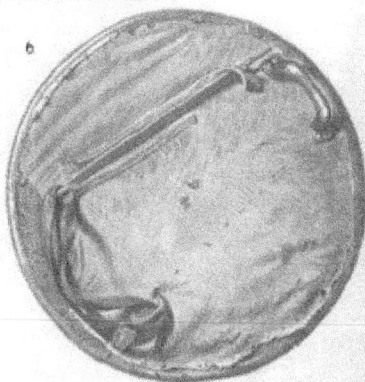

PLATE II.—TARGETS

Fig

HIGHLAND TARGET OF WOOD AND LEATHER, with central boss, surrounded 1
by four smaller bosses, placed alternately with four diamond-shaped plates of
thin brass. The boss forms the centre of a star of four points, in each of which is a
heart-shaped plate of thin brass. The quadrants of the circle in which the star is
placed have each a scroll-like ornament tooled in the leather. A running scroll of
foliageous ornament occupies the outer margin of the shield.

HIGHLAND TARGET OF WOOD AND LEATHER, richly ornamented with scroll-work and 2
circles filled with geometrical figures and interlaced work. The boss occupies the
centre of a quatrefoil. The quadrants of the circle in which the quatrefoil is placed
are filled with fine scroll-work, and the space between the central circles and the
margin of the shield is filled with circles enclosing quatrefoils, rosettes, and patterns
of interlaced work.

HIGHLAND TARGET OF WOOD AND LEATHER, having a central boss surrounded by six 3
smaller bosses, in circles of scroll-work tooled in the leather. One of the smaller
bosses is shown on an enlarged scale in the space above.

HIGHLAND TARGET OF WOOD AND LEATHER, having no boss; the centre ornamented with 4
a stud and four nails, and the surface covered with foliageous scroll-work, arranged
in the quadrants of the circle of the shield, divided by a star of four rays reaching
from the centre to the circumference. This target is in the Perth Museum.

HIGHLAND TARGET OF WOOD AND LEATHER, with central boss, surrounded by a circle of 5
geometric ornament. A similar ornament is repeated in two concentric bands between
the central circle and the outer margin of the shield.

HIGHLAND TARGET OF WOOD AND LEATHER, with central boss, surrounded by a circle of 6
interlaced work, arranged in patterns in the quadrants of the circle. The space between
the central circle and the outer margin is occupied by concentric circles similarly
divided. The inner of these two circular bands is filled with foliageous scroll-work
with studs in the openings, and the outer with patterns of interlaced work, having
studs in the openings. This target is preserved at Castle Grant.

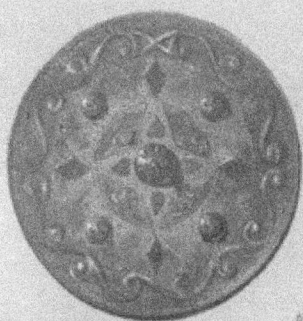

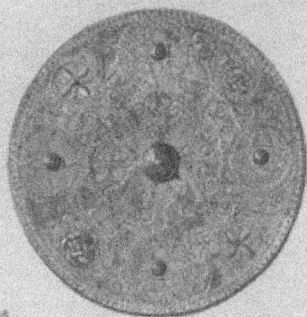

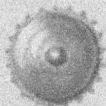

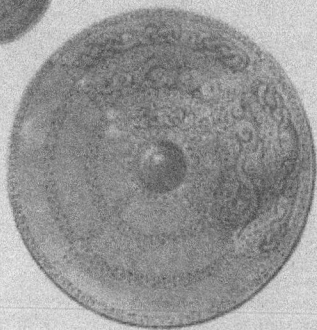

PLATE III.—TARGETS

Fig

HIGHLAND TARGET OF WOOD AND LEATHER, 20 inches diameter, and 1 slightly concave in the surface. It has no boss, the centre being occupied by a rosette in the middle of a four-rayed star; the quadrants of the circle in which the star is placed being filled with scroll-work. Round the central circle is a circular band, with a running scroll and studs. The band between this and the outer margin is divided into spaces alternately triangular and semi-circular. In each of the semi-circular spaces is a nondescript animal, faintly outlined. This target is in the National Museum of Antiquities, Edinburgh.

HIGHLAND TARGET OF WOOD AND LEATHER, 21 inches diameter, having no boss, but in 2 the centre a star surrounded by concentric bands alternately of interlaced work and foliageous scrolls. In the Tower Armoury, London.

HIGHLAND TARGET OF WOOD AND LEATHER, with central boss in a circle of scroll-work, 3 surrounded by four circles with central studs and convoluted scrolls. The spaces between the circles are occupied by interlaced work, scroll-like ornaments, and triangular figures enclosing hearts. This target belonged to the late Keith Stewart Mackenzie of Seaforth.

BACK OF TARGET, showing its lining of skin and remains of the sleeve of leather. 4

HIGHLAND TARGET OF WOOD AND LEATHER, with central boss, surrounded by a circle of 5 scroll-work, and a concentric band of triangular ornaments of thin brass. Beyond these are concentric bands of interlaced work arranged in narrow panels.

HIGHLAND TARGET OF WOOD AND LEATHER, with central boss, from which a hexafoil 6 extends to the circumference, simply outlined in the leather and ornamented with nail-heads.

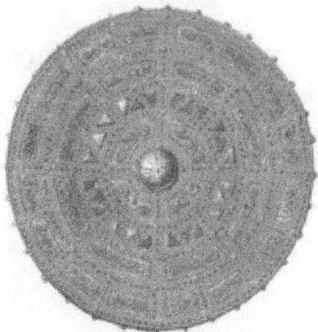

PLATE IV.—TARGETS

HIGHLAND TARGET of wood and leather, ornamented with nails, studs, and a central boss of brass. Round the boss is a circle, surrounded by four smaller circles of nail-heads with central studs placed in the angles of a square. The whole surrounded by another circle of nail-heads, intersected by four smaller circles, with central studs alternating with four triangles, the apices of which touch the outer circle of nail-heads within the margin of the shield. **1**

HIGHLAND TARGET of wood and leather, ornamented with nails, studs, and segmental plates of thin brass, and having a central boss of brass, furnished with an iron spike. The ornamentation consists of a series of six circles, enclosing triangles arranged round the central circle, a segmental plate coming between each pair of circles, and the whole enclosed within a marginal border, consisting of a double row of nail-heads. **2**

HIGHLAND TARGET of wood and leather, ornamented with nails and segmental plates of thin brass, and having a central boss, surrounded by six smaller bosses. The design of the ornament consists of six circles arranged tangentially round a central circle, each having a central boss, with open work, showing a lining of crimson cloth. Four lozenge-shaped segmental plates radiate cross-wise from the circumference of the bosses. The spaces between the circles are filled by segmental plates, and the whole enclosed in a marginal border of a single row of nail-heads. This target is in the collection of Mr Gourlay Steell, R.S.A. **3**

BACK OF TARGET, showing its lining of skin, with the handle of iron, and arm-strap of leather. **4**

HIGHLAND TARGET of wood and leather, with bosses of brass. The whole surface is ornamented with patterns of interlaced work and foliageous scrolls tooled in the leather, and arranged in circular and triangular spaces, bordered by rows of small nail-heads. **5**

BACK OF TARGET, showing its lining of skin, with handle and arm-strap of leather. **6**

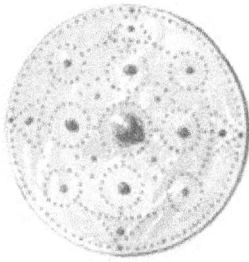

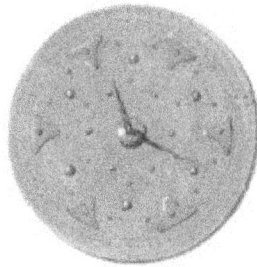

3

4

5

6

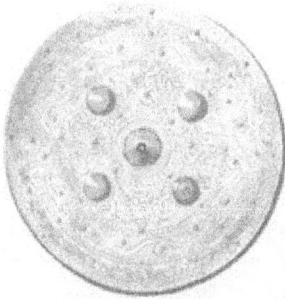

PLATE V.—TARGETS

H IGHLAND TARGET of wood, covered with leather, and ornamented with a central boss and studs of brass. Round the boss is a circular space bordered, and divided into quadrants, by double rows of nails. In this circle the leather is tooled with patterns of interlaced work and scroll-work, and intermingled with the ornament are the initials and date, " D. M'L., 1723." The exterior space is also divided into quadrants, in each of which are two arcs of circles filled with scrolls of different patterns tooled in the leather. A double row of nails surrounds the whole, and the edge of the target is ornamented with brass studs. **1**

HIGHLAND TARGET of wood and leather, with central boss of brass, pierced for a spike. The inner circle round the boss contains the name and date, " D. M'Leod, 1719." The outer circle is filled with a repeating pattern, consisting of a semi-circular space divided into three compartments—the middle compartment filled with a triquetra, the others with fleurs-de-lis. These spaces alternate with rosettes in circles surrounded by scrolls. In the drawing only part of the ornament is given. **2**

HIGHLAND TARGET of wood and leather, with central boss pierced for a spike. Round the boss (which is shown separately in Fig. b) is a circle of interlaced work tooled in the leather. In the exterior space are six equal circles, each with a central stud of brass, and round it three smaller circles, the spaces between them filled with interlacements. The spaces between the larger circles are filled with segmental plates of brass fastened with nails and studs, as shown at Fig. d. The large Fig. A shows the target in profile, with the spike in its socket. The back of the target is given as Fig. 7 in Plate I. The small bosses are shown under Fig. c. This target is the property of Col. R. Stewart of Ardvoirlich, Perthshire. **3**

BACK OF TARGET, with handle and sleeve of leather instead of the usual arm-band or strap. **4**

HIGHLAND TARGET of wood and leather. It has no boss, but shows the iron socket for the spike. The plan of its ornamentation is similar to that of No. 3, except that the segmental plates between the circles are pierced and implanted upon red cloth, as shown at Fig c. This target is in the National Museum of Antiquities, Edinburgh. **5**

HIGHLAND TARGET of wood and leather, with a central boss of brass, of which only a fragment remains. Round the boss is a six-rayed star with small circles between its points, the whole enclosed within a double circle of nail-heads. The space between these and the circumference of the target is divided into two circular bands of nearly equal width, the inner filled with interlaced work tooled in the leather; six rosettes of brass are placed on it at equal distances, and the whole enclosed within a double circle of nail-heads. The outer band has pierced triangular plates and quatrefoils of brass alternately, the spaces between them filled with a pattern of foliage tooled in the leather. Figures of the rosettes, triangular plates and quatrefoils are given separately. This target is said to have belonged to one of the Campbells of Jura, and is now in the collection of Mr Gourlay Steell, R.S.A. **6**

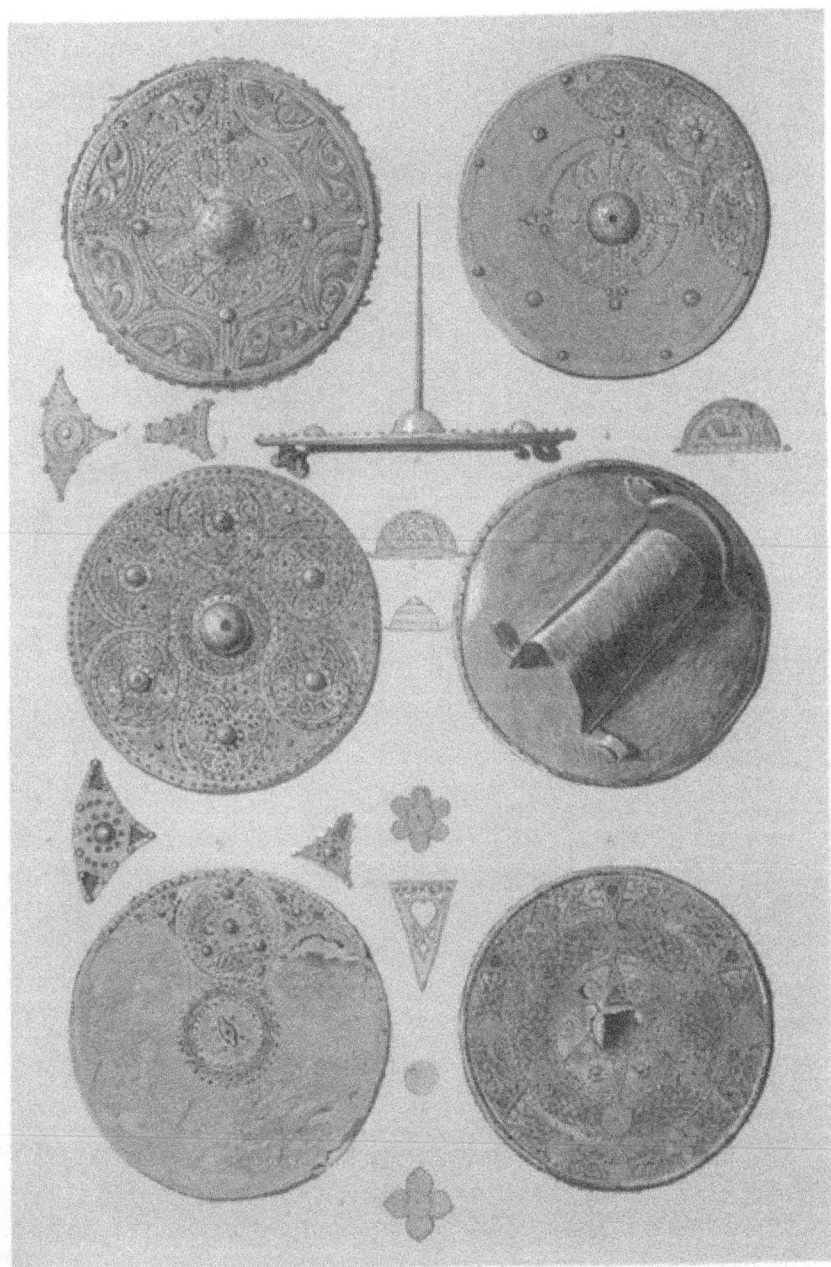

PLATE VI.—TARGETS

Fig

HIGHLAND TARGET of wood and leather, having no boss, but elaborately 1
ornamented with studs and nail-heads, and patterns tooled in the leather. In the
centre is a rosette. The circular band surrounding it is divided by segmental and
radiating lines into a peculiar pattern of symmetrically recurring segmental spaces filled
with radiating lines. The space between this circle and the circumference of the target is
occupied by four circles alternating with four diamond-shaped figures outlined by nail-
heads. The circles are filled with intricate patterns of interlaced work tooled in the
leather, and the spaces between them and the diamond-shaped figures are occupied by
foliage and scrolls similarly tooled.

HIGHLAND TARGET of wood and leather, with eight bosses of brass surrounding a central 2
boss, and simply decorated with rows of nail-heads.

HIGHLAND TARGET of wood and leather, with central boss of brass. The surface of the 3
target is divided into three concentric bands of nearly equal width, each ornamented
with different patterns tooled in the leather. In the space round the boss the ornament
consists of an interlacement from which the ends of the bands escape and terminate in
scrolls. The two outer circular bands are each divided into quadrants, which in the one
case are filled with scrolls, and in the other with patterns of interlaced work of great
beauty.

IRON or STEEL SHIELD, plain, with raised circular edging ornamented with nail-heads. 4

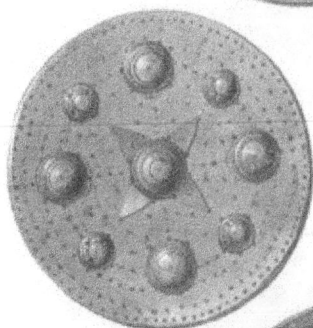

PLATE VII.—TARGETS

R EMAINS OF A SUPPOSED SHIELD OF OAK, 2 feet long, 19 inches broad   1
    at the widest part, but the breadth incomplete, 1¾ inches in thickness, but
thinning towards the outer edge where it is about 1 inch in thickness. It is composed of three pieces of wood morticed together longitudinally. The centre is wanting,
but there are two pieces of wood hollowed circularly, which Mr Drummond thought
might be the remains of the boss. Found in Blair Drummond Moss, and now in
the National Museum of Antiquities, Edinburgh.

SHIELD OF THIN BRONZE, 24 inches diameter, with a central boss, the surface ornamented   2
with concentric rings and with circular rows of studs between the rings, all beaten up
from the back; the edge a larger ring, beaten out and turned over. In the centre of
the shield, at the back of the boss, which is 4 inches diameter, a handle of the
same metal is fixed straight across the hollow and rivetted at both ends. Midway
between the centre and the rim, on either side of the boss, there are two tongues of
bronze about an inch in length moving on a pin at one end. These have been
supposed to be for the attachment of a strap for suspension. This shield was found
with another of similar form and character in a piece of marshy ground at Yetholm,
Roxburghshire. Both are now in the National Museum of Antiquities, Edinburgh.

HIGHLAND TARGET OF WOOD AND LEATHER, 20 inches in diameter, with a central boss   3
pierced for a spike. Round the boss is a circle tooled in the leather and studded
with nail-heads. In the space between the circumference of this circle and the margin
of the target are four similar circles at equal distances, alternating with triangular
plates of pierced brass, in pairs placed point to point. The property of John Steuart,
of Dalguise, deposited in the National Museum of Antiquities, Edinburgh.

HIGHLAND TARGET OF WOOD AND LEATHER, 19 inches in diameter. It has no boss; the   4
centre being occupied by a small circular plate of thin brass 1½ inches diameter,
secured in the centre by a stud. A circle, 4 inches diameter, formed of a strip of
thin brass, surrounds the centre, and between the circumference of this circle and the
outer margin of the target is another circle vandyked as a star of eight points. The
spaces between the circles and the points of the star are ornamented with groups of
nail-heads symmetrically arranged, and the rim of the target is bound with an edging
of thin brass. The property of John Steuart, of Dalguise, deposited in the National
Museum of Antiquities, Edinburgh.

[This plate having been left by Mr Drummond incomplete, Nos. 2, 3, and 4 have
been drawn from the originals by Mr William Gibb.]

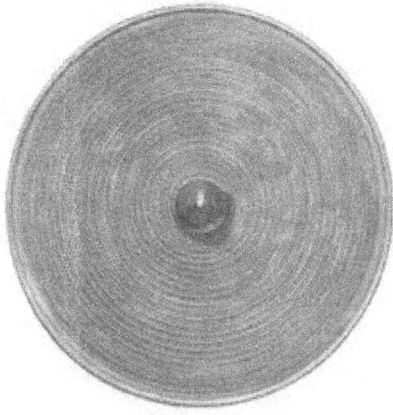

PLATE VIII.—SWORDS

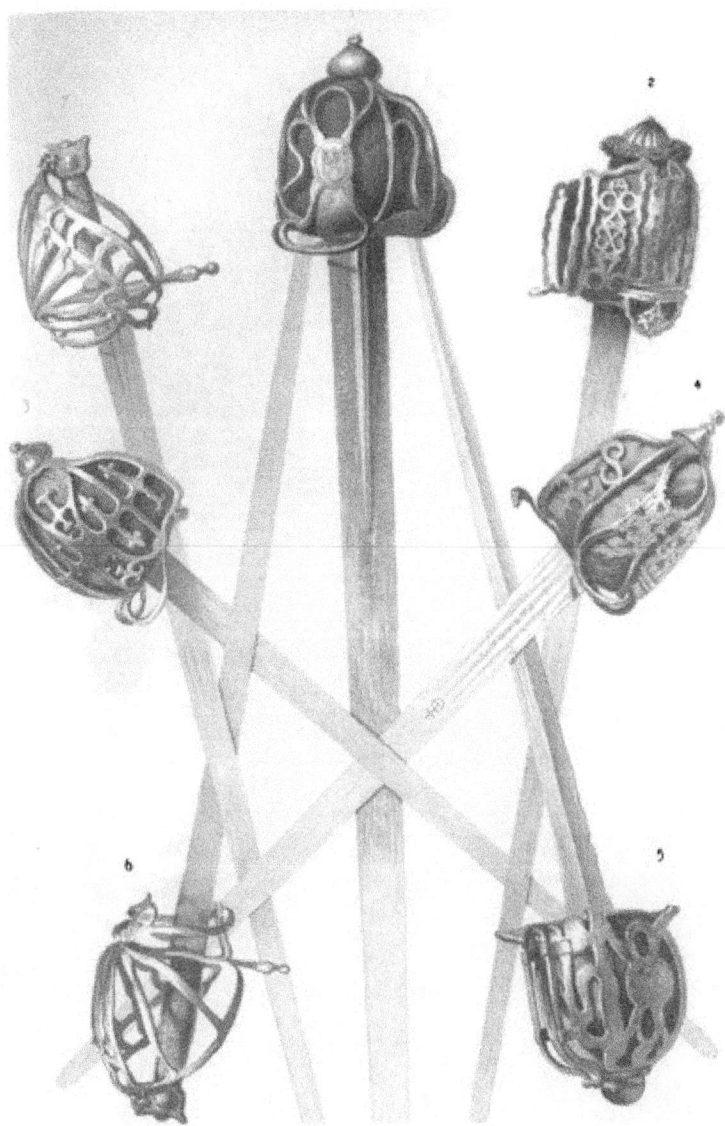

PLATE IX.—SWORDS

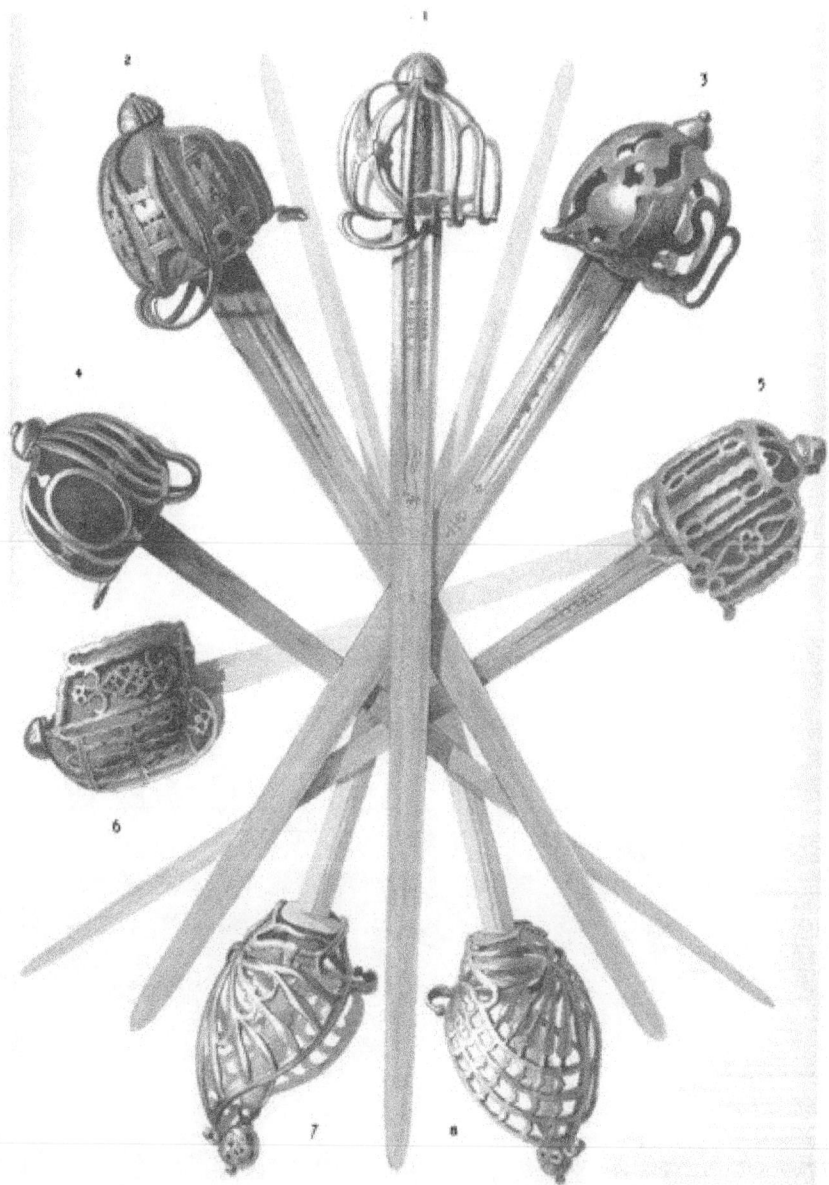

PLATE X.—SWORDS

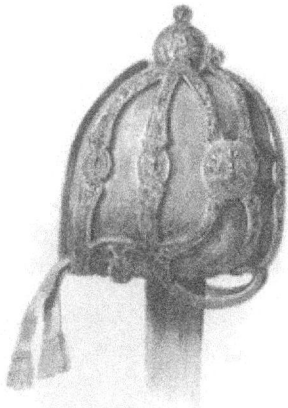

3

4

PLATE XI.—TWO-HANDED SWORDS

PLATE XII.—TWO-HANDED SWORDS

Fig.

TWO-HANDED SWORD, with globular pommel, the mounting of the grip gone, the guard recurved towards the point, the blade 3 feet 7 inches in length. In the National Museum of Antiquities, Edinburgh.   1

Two-Handed Sword, with globular pommel, the grip slightly swelling in the middle, the guard long and straight, with pierced ornamental terminations, and side rings, the blade 4 feet 1 inch in length. In the National Museum of Antiquities, Edinburgh.   2

Two-Handed Sword, with globular pommel and slightly swelling grip, 15 inches in length; the guard short, but having its ends strongly recurved towards the point; the blade 3 feet 7 inches in length. In the National Museum of Antiquities, Edinburgh.   3

Two-Handed Sword, with globular pommel, the grip 21 inches long, slightly increasing in thickness from the pommel to the blade, and covered with leather bound with wire; the guard, which is furnished with side rings, bent slightly back towards the pommel, and the ends strongly recurved towards the points; the blade 3 feet 9 inches in length. In the National Museum of Antiquities, Edinburgh.   4

Two-Handed Sword, with globular pommel, the grip 22 inches long, increasing in size from the pommel to the blade, and covered with leather bound spirally with wire; the guard furnished with side rings, and strongly recurved towards the point; the blade 4 feet 3 inches in length. In the National Museum of Antiquities, Edinburgh.   5

Two-Handed Sword, with globular pommel, the grip 18 inches in length and ornamented in the middle; the guard ornamented with scrolls, strongly recurved towards the point, and furnished with ornamental side rings; the blade contracted in width in the upper part for 9 inches, and at that distance from the guard furnished with hooks, a common Swiss or German form of sixteenth century; the blade beyond the hooks 3 feet 4 inches in length.   6

Two-Handed Sword, with jewelled pommel, the grip swelling in the middle and ornamented with gilt studs; the guard strongly recurved towards the point, with ornamental terminations and hooks.   7

Two-Handed Sword, with circular pommel, the grip mounted with wood and leather, the guard recurved towards the point and ornamented with engraved lines.   8

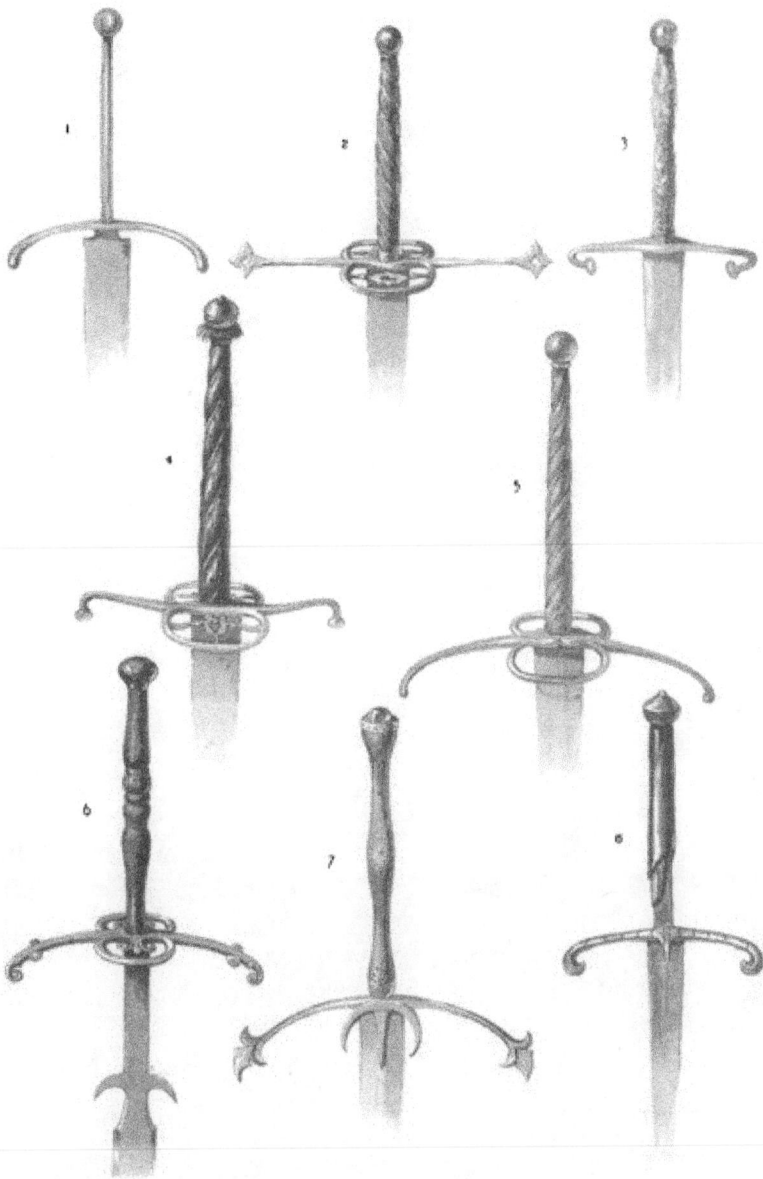

PLATE XIII.—TWO-HANDED SWORDS

TWO-HANDED SWORD, with long, narrow, and waved blade and hooks, cross- 1
guard and side rings, the ends of the quillons ornamented like scallop shells, and
bent to right and left; the grip divided by a swelling in the middle, and the pommel
terminating in a slightly swelling knob.

Two-Handed Sword, with slightly open guard, the quillons curving towards the point 2
and terminating in knobs, the grip covered with leather, and the pommel polygonal.

Two-Handed Sword, with broad blade, the guard slightly reversed, and the quillons 3
terminating in knobs; the grip slightly swelling in the middle, and the pommel globular.

Two-Handed Sword, with broad blade and shell guard, the quillons strongly curved 4
towards the point, and ending in open lozenge-shaped expansions, the grip swelling
slightly to the middle, and the pommel lobed and pear-shaped, ending in a button.

Two-Handed Sword, with stout blade and hooks, curved towards the hilt, the guard 5
straight and terminating in knobs, the grip diminishing from the guard to the pommel.

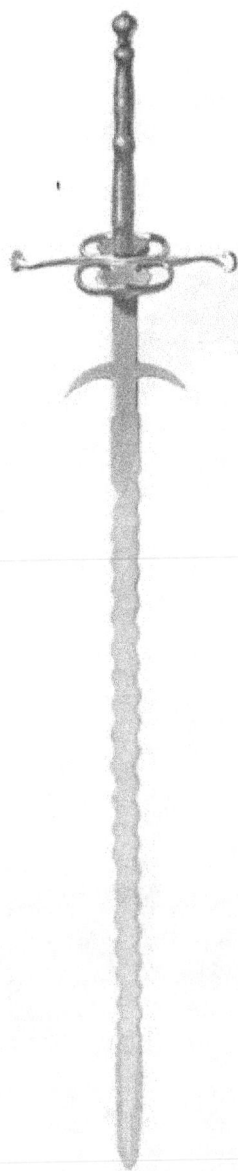

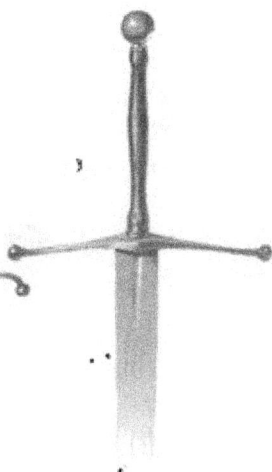

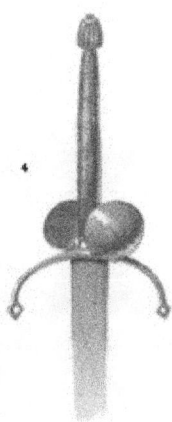

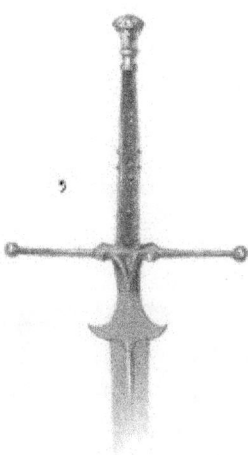

PLATE XIV.—SWORD AND SWORD HILTS

Fig.

SWORD, with slightly tapering double-edged blade 3 feet 7 inches in length, and 1 shell-guard, the quillons curved towards the point, the grip nearly cylindrical, the pommel globose, and terminating in a button or knob. In the National Museum of Antiquities, Edinburgh.

HILT of a large broad-bladed sword, with curved guard, the quillons bent towards the 2 point, the grip slightly swelling in the middle, the pommel wheel-shaped.

HILT of sword, with straight guard, the grip nearly cylindrical, the pommel globular, 3 and terminating in a button or knob.

HILT of a large broad-bladed sword, with straight guard, the grip nearly cylindrical, the 4 pommel conical.

HILT of sword, with short straight guard terminating in knobs, the grip slightly swelling 5 in the middle, the pommel conical.

HILT of large broad-bladed sword, the guard placed at right angles with the median 6 line of the blade, and bent to right and left at the opposite extremities, the grip tapering to the top, the pommel flattened. This sword is in the collection of Sir J. Noel Paton, in whose "Private Catalogue" it is thus described:—"Early Venetian sword, with flat square pommel, cross-guard reversely bent, original grip of tooled leather; its very broad blade bears traces of engraving. Several identical swords are preserved in the arsenal at Venice." The drawing is unfinished.

HILT of large broad-bladed sword, with massive straight guard, the grip cylindrical, and 7 the top of the pommel flat.

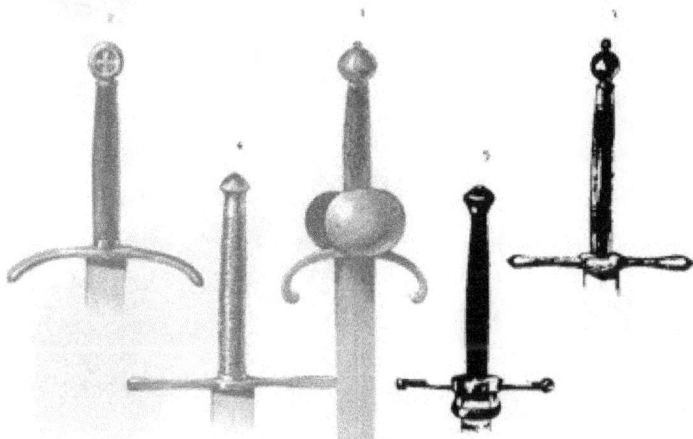

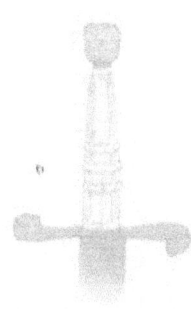

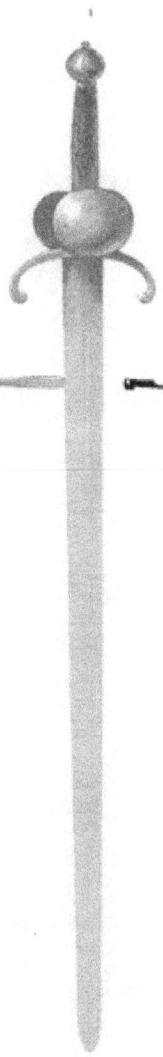

PLATE XV—TWO-HANDED SWORDS

TWO-HANDED SCOTTISH SWORD, with short grip, small globular pommel, 1 and reversed guard; the quillons angularly inclined towards the point of the weapon, and terminating in a quatrefoil of open circles.

Two-Handed Scottish Sword, with heavier blade and grip, 12⅜ inches in length to 2 extremity of pommel; the pommel rounded and flattened, terminating in a button; the quillons of the guard inclined towards the point, and terminating in quatrefoils of open circles, one of which is wanting; the blade 3 feet 3 inches in length. This sword is in the collection of Sir J. Noel Paton.

Two-Handed Scottish Sword, with globular pommel and reversed guard, the grip 3 12 inches in length, the mounting partly gone; the quillons of the guard inclined at an angle towards the point, and terminating in quatrefoils of open circles; the blade 3 feet 6 inches in length.

Two-Handed Scottish Sword, with semi-globular slightly conical pommel, the grip 4 swelling in the middle, and the quillons of the guard slightly inclined towards the point, and terminating in quatrefoils of open circles.

Two-Handed Scottish Sword, with lengthened grip of ivory carved in a twisted form; 5 the pommel rounded and flattened on two sides, with a terminal button; the guard double, or having four quillons inclined towards the point, and terminating in quatrefoils of open circles. This sword is preserved at Hawthornden, Midlothian.

Two-Handed Scottish Sword, with flat circular pommel and terminal button, the grip 6 slightly swelling, the quillons greatly and unequally inclined towards the point, and terminating in quatrefoils of open circles.

Two-Handed Scottish Sword, with globular pommel, and lengthened grip swelling in 7 the upper part; the quillons of the guard greatly inclined towards the point, and terminating in quatrefoils of open circles; the blade wide and heavy, with prominent midrib. On either side of the midrib on the upper part of the blade is the inscription in two lines.

> " I WILL VENTER SELFE IN BATEL STRONG
> TO VINDICATE MY MASTERS WRONG."

Two-Handed Scottish Sword, with pommel rounded and grip swelling in the middle, 8 the quillons of the guard slightly inclined towards the point, and terminating in quatrefoils of open circles.

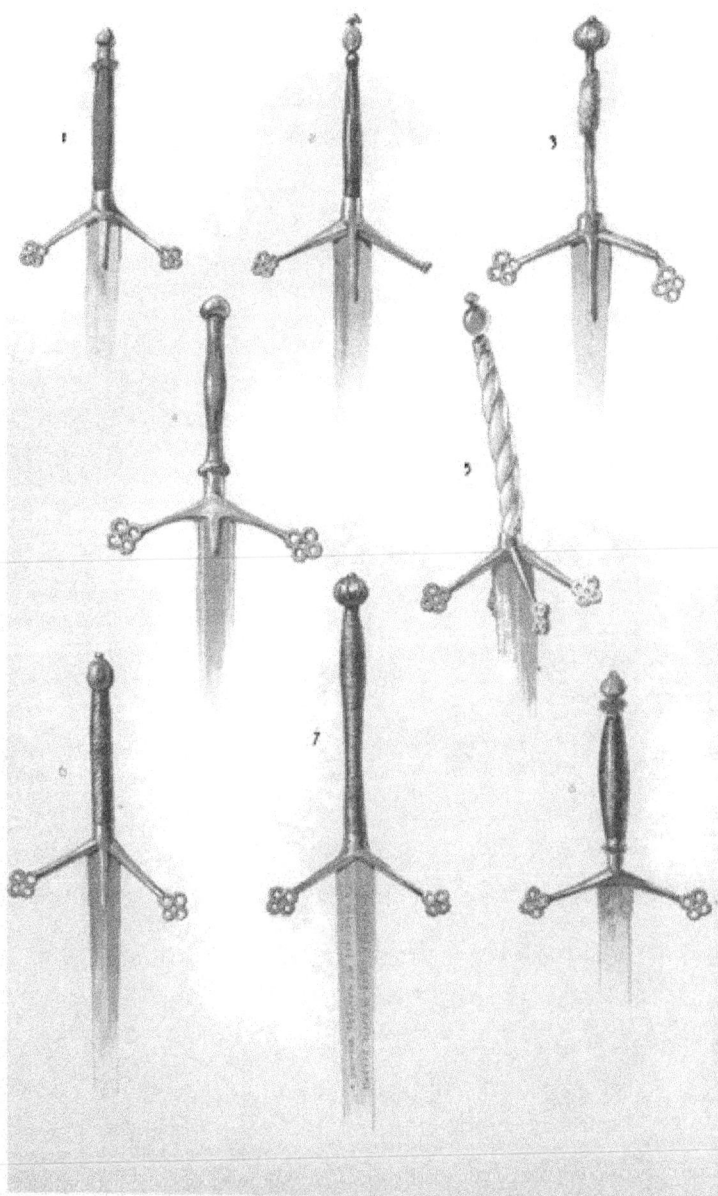

PLATE XVI.—SWORD AND SWORD HILTS

SWORD, with slightly tapering double-edged blade 34 inches in length, 1¼ inches 1
wide at the junction with the hilt, and ⅜ inch wide at the point; the guard reversed;
the quillons 3½ inches in length, and 6 inches apart at their tips; the grip 3½ inches in
length, its mounting gone; the pommel wheel-shaped, 2 inches diameter. In the
National Museum of Antiquities, Edinburgh.

HILT OF A BROAD-BLADED, DOUBLE-EDGED SWORD; the blade 2 inches wide at the junction 2
with the hilt; the guard 3½ inches in length, flattened and curved towards the point; the
grip 3½ inches in length, its mounting gone; no pommel, but merely a smaller reversed
guard on the extremity of the tang of the blade. Dug up from a depth of 6 feet, in
gravel, at Ballaugh, Isle of Man, in 1824, and now in the National Museum of
Antiquities, Edinburgh.

HILT OF A LARGE SWORD, with double-edged blade 1½ inches wide at the junction with the 3
hilt; the guard 18 inches in length, flattened and curved towards the point; the grip 5
inches in length; the pommel wheel-shaped, 2 inches in diameter. In the National
Museum of Antiquities, Edinburgh.

HILT OF A LARGE SWORD, with double-edged blade, 2 inches wide at the junction with the 4
hilt; the guard 12 inches in length, and straight; the grip 6½ inches long; the pommel
flattened. In the National Museum of Antiquities, Edinburgh.

HUNTING SWORD, single-edged; the edge waved; the hilt quaintly made of deer horn. 5

HILT OF A HUNTING SWORD, with double-edged blade; the grip and cross-guard quaintly 6
mounted with the burrs of deer-horns.

HILT OF A HUNTING SWORD, with broad double-edged blade, and finger-guard of brass, highly 7
ornamented, and terminating in a grotesque animal's head.

SWORD, with broad, heavy, double-edged blade, measuring 31⅞ inches in length, from guard 8
to point, 2¼ inches wide at the junction with the hilt, and slightly tapering to 1⅜ inches
at the point; the blade damascened; the guard 5 inches in length, 1 inch wide, and ⅜
inch thick, curved towards the point, and ornamented with inlaying of silver; the grip
3½ inches in length; the pommel tri-lobed in form, and also ornamented with inlaying in
silver. Found in excavating a cutting on the Strathspey Railway, at Gorton, in Moray-
shire, and now in the National Museum of Antiquities, Edinburgh.

HILT OF A LARGE, BROAD-BLADED, AND DOUBLE-EDGED SWORD, with basket guard, and globular 9
pommel.

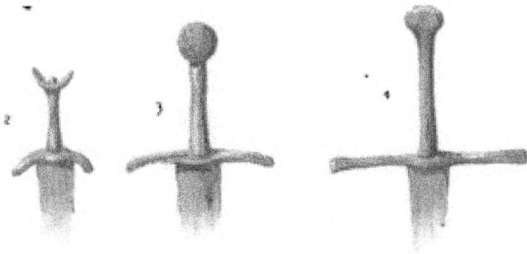

PLATE XVII.—DIRKS

Fig

S MALL HIGHLAND DIRK, with plain handle, the grip tapering and curved, and   1
slightly shouldered at its junction with the blade.

SMALL DAGGER, with tapering handle and cross-guard with knobs.   2

HIGHLAND DIRK, with buckhorn handle and sheath of leather, tooled with interlaced work,   3
and having side sheaths for knife and fork.

ANCIENT SCOTTISH DIRK, with wooden handle knobbed at the end, the grip nearly of equal   4
width throughout, but strongly shouldered at the insertion of the blade. Found with
a knife-blade of iron in a grave at East Langton, Midlothian, in 1852, and now in
the National Museum of Antiquities, Edinburgh.

HIGHLAND DIRK, with finely carved handle; the grip short and swelling, the shouldered   5
part unusually long, and both covered with carved interlacements; the cap of brass,
and flat-topped, with four conical projections.

SMALL KNIFE-DAGGER, with rounded tapering handle, knobbed at the end, and having four   6
projections like No. 5.

DIRK, knife-shaped, with slight guard and tapering handle, carved with closely worked   7
interlacements.

HIGHLAND DIRK in its sheath, with side sheaths for knife and fork; the dirk, knife and   8
fork, and the cap of the dirk handle also shown separately. The blade of the dirk
has a groove near the back, pierced by ten holes at regular intervals.

> Over No. 8 is a beautifully carved Dirk Handle, of Highland form, the cap flat-topped, the grip
> slightly swelling and deeply shouldered, and the whole covered with a regular pattern of
> interlaced work. In the National Museum of Antiquities, Edinburgh.

HIGHLAND DIRK, the blade much corroded, and the buckhorn handle shouldered and capped   9
with mountings of Brass.

HIGHLAND DIRK, with handle of bone or ivory, the cap and shoulder plain, the grip carved   10
with lines spirally twisted.

LARGE HIGHLAND DIRK in its sheath, with side sheaths for knife and fork. The handle is   11
finely carved with interlaced work of serpents, the heads of which escape and appear
on the shoulder of the grip. The cap is flat-topped and silver-mounted. The knife
and fork handles are also carved with interlaced work, and silver-mounted. The sheath
is ornamented with leaves and heads of the thistle.

HIGHLAND DIRK, with finely carved handle. The grip is encircled with three bands of   12
interlacements, each of a different pattern, and the shoulder decorated with three triquetras.
The cap is of brass, flat-topped, with a stud in the centre. The blade, which is 12½ inches
in length, and 1½ inches in width, has a groove near the back pierced by three holes, and
between them and the shoulder of the grip there is a band of brass dovetailed and riveted
into the back of the blade, and finely engraved with scroll patterns. On one side of
the blade is engraved the inscription, "A SOFT ANSWER TOURNETH AWAY WRATH," and
on the other side the distich,

"THY KING AND COUNTRIES CAUSE DEFEND
THOUGH ON THE SPOT YOUR LIFE SHOULD END."

Bequeathed by Mr James Drummond, R.S.A., to the National Museum of Antiquities,
Edinburgh.

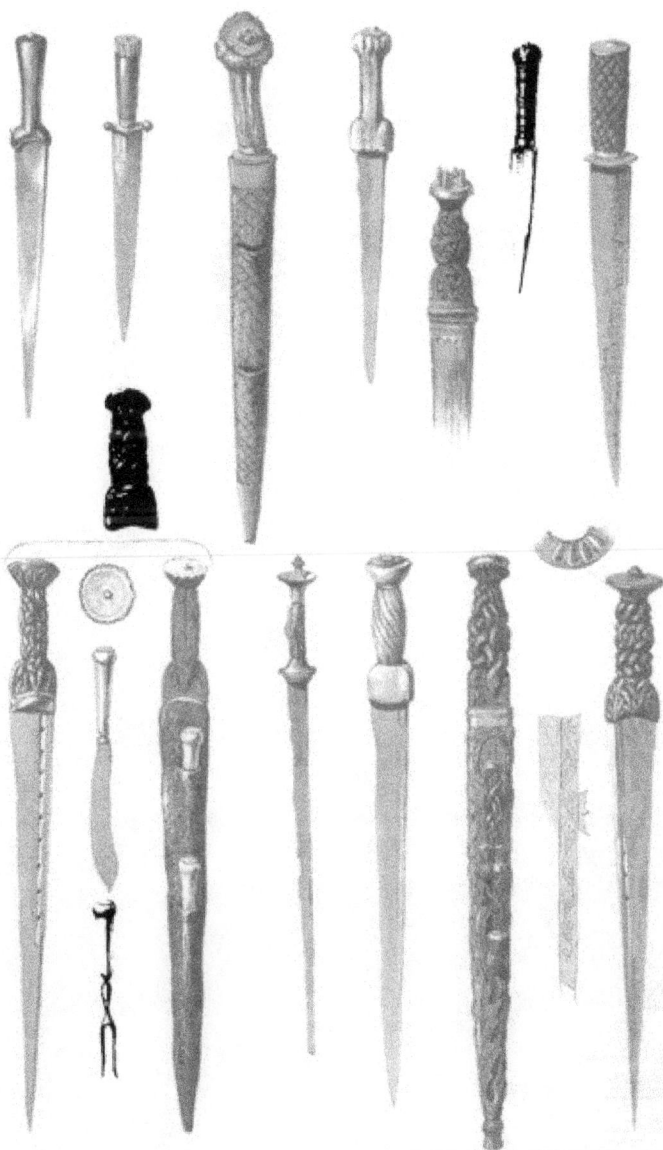

PLATE XVIII.—HIGHLAND DIRKS

Fig.

HIGHLAND DIRK, with handle of wood; the grip carved with patterns of   1
interlaced work; the pommel gone; the sheath of leather, with stamped ornament,
and mounting of brass, and a side-sheath for a knife.   Shown in different positions
as follows:—

(a) Front view of the Dirk, with the knife in its side-sheath, and the knife separately.

(b) Side view of the Dirk without the sheath, and view of the back of the Dirk,
showing an engraved inscription and date:—
"FEAR GOD AND DO NOT KIL, 1680."

(c) Side view of the Dirk in its sheath; the pommel restored.

HIGHLAND DIRK, with handle of wood; the grip carved with interlaced patterns, shouldered   2
where it meets the blade, and having a circular flat-topped pommel, ornamented with
a brass stud.

HIGHLAND DIRK, with handle of wood; the grip richly carved with interlaced patterns; the   3
lower part strongly shouldered; the upper constricted, and terminating in a circular
flat-topped pommel.

HIGHLAND DIRK; the blade longer and narrower than usual; the handle of wood; the grip   4
slightly shouldered and richly carved with interlacing patterns, and terminating in a
flat-topped pommel.

HIGHLAND DIRK, with richly carved handle, shown in two views, viz.:—   5
Side view of the Dirk without the sheath; the blade is double-edged and
probably not the original.
View of the Dirk, with its sheath, showing side-loop for suspension.

HIGHLAND DIRK, with handle of wood; the grip strongly shouldered and richly carved   6
with interlaced work, terminating in a circular flat-topped pommel with central stud of
brass.

HIGHLAND DIRK in its sheath, with side sheaths for knife and fork; the handles of wood   7
carved with interlacing patterns, and mounted with metal caps.

HIGHLAND DIRK (upper part only); the handle of wood, carved with interlaced work; the   8
lower part slightly shouldered; the pommel flat, circular, and mounted with brass.

HIGHLAND DIRK in its sheath, with side sheaths for knife and fork; the grip of the handle   9
swelling in the middle and richly carved with interlaced work; the pommel flat,
circular, and mounted with brass.

HIGHLAND DIRK, with narrow blade, in its sheath, with side sheaths for knife and fork;   10
the handles of wood, and finely carved with interlaced work; the grip of the dirk
strongly shouldered, and richly carved; the pommel flat, circular, and its brass
mounting ornamented with a central stud and four circles.

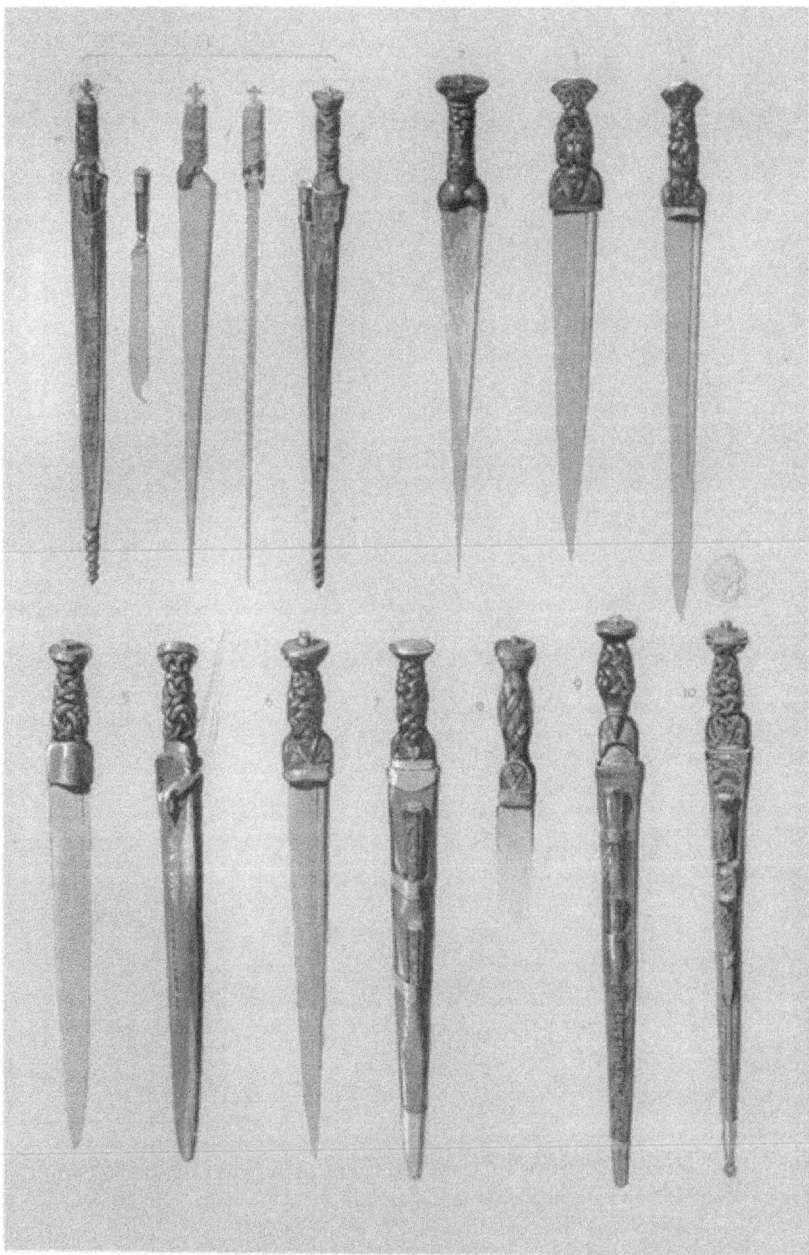

PLATE XIX.—HIGHLAND DIRKS

[This plate, having been left by Mr Drummond incomplete, Nos. 5, and 8-12 inclusive,
have been drawn from the originals by Mr William Gibb.]

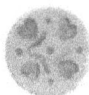

PLATE XX.—POWDER HORNS

Fig.

FLATTENED POWDER HORN, 14 inches in length, richly engraved with scrolls of foliage and a hunting scene, and bearing also a complicated monogram which Mr Drummond regarded as that of Sir George Mackenzie of Tarbat, who succeeded his father in the baronetcy in 1654. The engraving on the horn represents two deer-hounds pursuing two stags into a thicket, while two huntsmen on foot appear in the background. The principal figure is dressed in a slashed jerkin of the time of Charles I., a vandyke frill, and a flat bonnet with feather. A deer-hound, held in leash, stands in front of him, and partly conceals the remaining portions of his dress, which are, however, described by Mr Drummond as consisting of the belted plaid and trews, for "though the deer-hound stands before him yet his legs are seen above the knees and are chequered as far as seen." He carries a gun on his shoulder, a powder horn slung at his side, and a dirk suspended from his belt. His attendant is bare-headed, and wears a deer-skin jerkin, kilt or belted plaid with sporran and chequered hose, tabbed at the top and scarcely reaching to the knee. He is blowing a horn held in the left hand, while the right grasps his master's gun-rest. A hooded falcon is perched in the scroll of foliage in front of them, and below the monogram are two birds fighting. This horn is now in the National Museum of Antiquities at Edinburgh with the other articles bequeathed by Mr Drummond.

PLAN of the convex edge of the horn showing its decoration of interlaced work and foliageous scrolls.

REVERSE OF THE SAME HORN, richly decorated with interlaced work of complicated design. It shows also the loop left on the edge of the horn for the string, carved in the shape of a human head.

PLAN of the interlaced decoration of the concave edge of the horn.

1

2

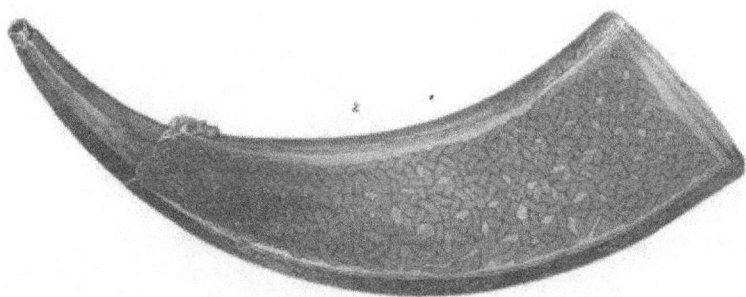

PLATE XXI.—POWDER HORNS

FLAT POWDER HORN, narrow and greatly curved ; the lower part stained red and 1
ornamented with a figure of a centaur, having a bow in the left hand and a serpent
in the right. Behind the centaur is a fortress, with a banner on the central tower.
The upper part of the horn is ornamented with a wavy foliageous scroll and an
aquatic monster. On the concave edge of the horn is the inscription REBVS
IVNGENDA SAPIENTIA. The inscription is blundered in the spelling, and the
words are improperly divided. This horn is in the Museum at Perth, and is said to
have belonged to the Duke of Perth. It is probably of Continental manufacture.

REVERSE OF THE SAME HORN, similarly decorated, but having at the lower end, and 2
within a floriated scroll, a figure of the brazen serpent, and below it, on a plain scroll,
the letters W T. I A. Over the serpent is a crown, to its right a windmill, and
to its left a castle. On the scroll enclosing this group of devices is the inscription,
CRVCE CORONO ET + SVPERATA.

1

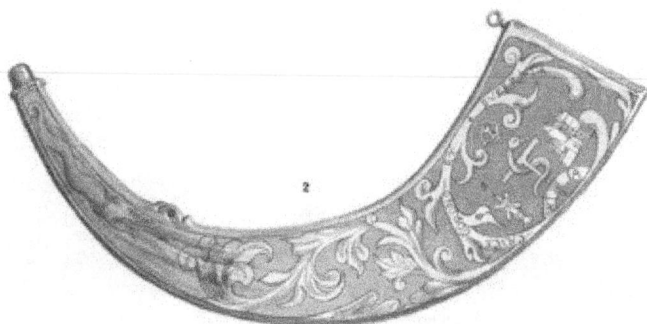

2

PLATE XXII.—POWDER-HORNS

No

FLAT HIGHLAND POWDER-HORN, with loop in the butt end and loop on the   1
inner side, near the mouth, for the cord by which it was slung. The flat side of the
Horn is decorated with four circles, filled with engraved patterns of interlaced and
geometric ornament. On the plain part, near the small end, are the initials I. B.
A Powder-Horn, with ornamentation precisely similar to this, and with the same
initials, but having an F inside the B, is in the Montrose Museum, and said to have
belonged to Francis Findlay, Ferryden, who was out at Culloden in the '45.

FLAT HIGHLAND POWDER-HORN, engraved with circles and bands of scale-like ornament.   2
In the larger circle are the initials A. R.   In the National Museum of Antiquities,
Edinburgh.

FLAT HIGHLAND POWDER-HORN, obverse and reverse sides of, 11½ inches in length. The   3
obverse side is entirely covered with bands of interlaced and geometric ornament finely
engraved. In two of the upper bands are the initials G. R. and the date 1685. The
reverse side has an ornamental band in the middle, and one at each end. Bequeathed
by Mr Drummond to the National Museum of Antiquities, Edinburgh.

FLAT HIGHLAND POWDER HORN, obverse and reverse sides of, both ornamented with circles   4
of geometric ornament. The obverse has the initials A. G. and a small equal-armed
cross with expanded ends. The reverse has the initials I. B.   The mouth of the Horn
is mounted with lead, and the inner edge has a side loop for a sling. Presented to the
National Museum of Antiquities, Edinburgh, by the late Mr Andrew Jervise, Brechin,
in 1855.

FLAT HIGHLAND POWDER-HORN, richly ornamented in the style of the later sculptured stone   5
crosses of the West Highlands. The lower part is filled with foliageous scroll-work.
At the upper end of the scrolls a bird sits in each loop of the inter-twisted stems. Above
are four animals arranged in a circle, and in a smaller circle a double-headed eagle
displayed. In the space between the circles are two grotesque faces. Above the circle
with the double-headed eagle are the initials C. M. L. and the date 1678. The details
of the ornament of the edges of the Horn are shown above it. The mountings are
modern. This Powder-Horn is now in the National Museum of Antiquities, Edinburgh,
and was formerly in the collection of the late Mr W. B. Johnstone.

FLAT POWDER-HORN, ornamented with a panel of rudely executed interlaced work.   6

FLAT POWDER-HORN, ornamented with engraved circles.   7

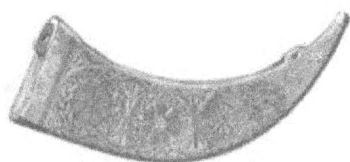

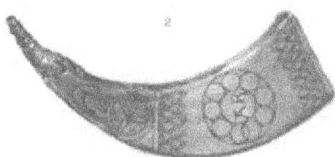

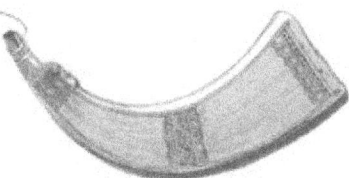

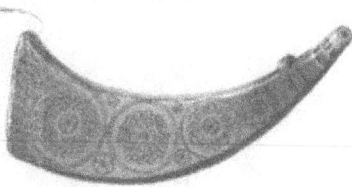

PLATE XXIII.—POWDER HORNS

Fig.

FLAT HIGHLAND POWDER HORN, 12 inches in length, obverse and reverse 1 sides of, both highly decorated with panels of interlaced work, and geometric ornament, engraved on the surface of the horn. It is furnished with two projecting loops at the butt, and two side loops near the mouth, for suspension. The conical part at the mouth of the horn is mounted with lead. The inner edge bears an inscription :—

"SEEK ME NOT I PRAY THE MY MESTER VIL DENEY ME FATLES

APRYL 4 YEAR OF GOD 1694

AND, BODY, FEAR GOD IN HEAY."

This horn is in the National Museum of Antiquities, Edinburgh.

FLAT HIGHLAND POWDER HORN, with brass mountings and rings for suspension. The 2 obverse side is decorated with interlaced and geometric ornament. The reverse bears a shield, surmounted by the letters I D, and surrounded by a circular border of geometric ornament. In a square panel is the inscription :—

" MEMORANDVM

NVLLI DANDVM

OB CAVSAM Q^DAM

NON SCIENDAM

NEC ROGANDAM

JVNE   3RD."

On the edge of the horn there is another inscription, as follows :—

"GIFT LIVETENAND WILLIAM GRANT OF AEWIE

TO IOHN DONALDSONE OF BOGSYDE 169   "

The last figure of the date is concealed by the brass mounting of the butt.

FLAT HIGHLAND POWDER HORN, with projecting side-loop carved into the form of a human 3 face. The mouth of the horn is closed by a stopper of wood. The obverse side is covered with finely engraved patterns of interlaced and geometric ornament, with the letters V T and a thistle-head in the upper panel. The reverse bears the lion and unicorn in the lower panel, with the letters V T, surrounded by an ornamental border ; the upper part of the horn is filled with foliageous ornament. One edge bears the owner's name, WILLIAM TVRNER, and the date 1679. The other edge has the inscription :—

"SIKE ME VITHIN VEIL POUDER."

FLAT HIGHLAND POWDER HORN, with side loop near the mouth for suspension, and 4 decorated with interlaced work and geometric ornament.

FLAT HIGHLAND POWDER HORN, obverse and reverse sides of, decorated with geometric 5 ornament, and having on the reverse a panel with the owner's initials, J D, and the date 1643.

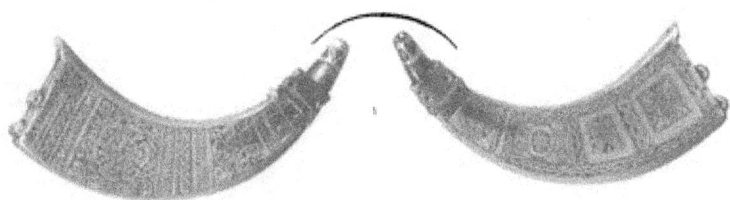

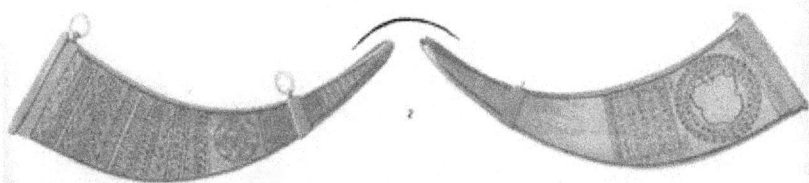

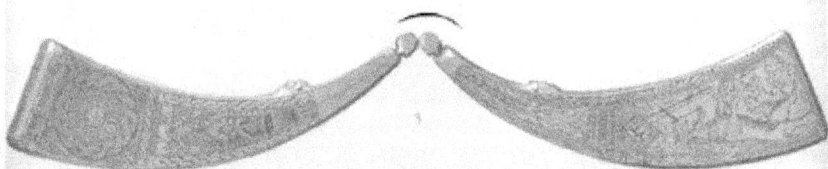

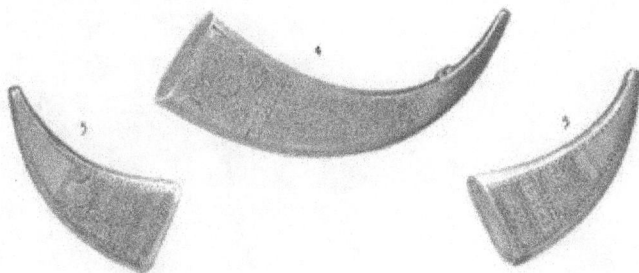

PLATE XXIV.—POWDER HORNS

Fig

POWDER HORN, having the edges carved with figures of animals in relief, and 1
the small end formed into the representation of an animal's mouth. The flat side
bears a representation of Judith with the head of Holofernes. In the panel below
are two lion-like animals, and a tree.

POWDER HORN, with brass mountings and spring mouthpiece fitted on the upper part of 2
the horn, which is shortened for the purpose of receiving it. The decoration is
simply a vandyked pattern of wavy lines with a double border.

POWDER HORN, of the same form as No. 2, but wanting the mouthpiece; the ends 3
ornamented with engraved patterns of interlaced work.

FLAT POWDER HORN, the obverse bearing a rose and thistle and floral scrolls; the reverse 4
shows the date 1690. The panel above the date shows a grotesque face, and that
below it has two heads facing each other in skull-caps, with turned up brims.

FLAT POWDER HORN, 9¼ inches in length, having the small end carved into the repre- 5
sentation of an animal's head. The obverse has the date 1708 within a floral scroll;
the reverse shows a smaller scroll and a stag running. In the National Museum of
Antiquities, Edinburgh.

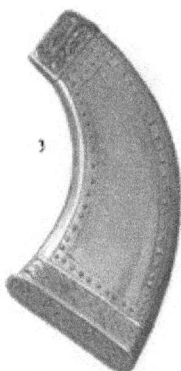

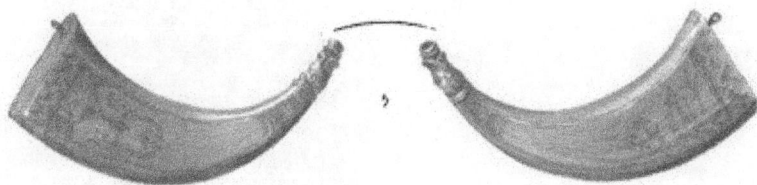

PLATE XXV.—POWDER HORNS

Fig.

FLAT HIGHLAND POWDER HORN, obverse and reverse sides; the obverse 1
ornamented with circles of interlaced work, a thistle, a *fleur-de-lis*, and a rude
representation of a man's head, surmounted by a flat broad-brimmed hat, the brims
turned up. Between the first and second circles is a shield of arms with supporters.
The reverse is less elaborately ornamented with geometric figures enclosed in circles
and bears the letters W L M K. In the collection of Sir J. Noel Paton, Kt. R.S.A.
In the "Private Catalogue" of that collection it is stated that it was found on the
field of Culloden immediately after the battle, and the following details are added:—
"The shield of arms bears a hart's head gorged, within a tressure *fleurie*, and is
surmounted by what seems to have been intended for a royal crown. The supporters
are: on the dexter side a unicorn gorged, bearing a banneret charged with a cross
saltire; on the sinister a hart also gorged, and bearing a banneret like the other
. . On the upper or concave edge of the horn are engraved two distichs:—

I LOVE THEE AS MY WYFFE   and ;—   A MAN HIS MYND SHOULD NEVER SET
I'LL KEEP THEE AS MY LYFFE.   UPON A THING HE CAN NOT GET.

with the date in large characters—1689. The interest of this fine Powder Horn is
increased by the fact that a portion of the original leather sling belt, closely studded
with brass studs, and with the original engraved brass buckle still remains."

FLAT HIGHLAND POWDER HORN, 8 inches in length, engraved with circles; the circles 2
and interspaces filled with geometric ornament. It bears on the upper part a thistle
and the date 1672, and has a man's face curiously inserted in the upper circle. In
the National Museum of Antiquities, Edinburgh.

FLAT HIGHLAND POWDER HORN, obverse and reverse sides. The obverse is elaborately 3
ornamented with alternate bands of interlaced work and geometric ornament, enclosed
within a border of interlaced work. The reverse is plain, with the exception of two
bands of ornament of a similar kind. The horn, which is 12½ inches in length,
retains the lead mounting of the mouth, and has a hole for suspension near the
small end. In the National Museum of Antiquities, Edinburgh.

[This plate having been left by Mr Drummond incomplete, Nos. 2 and 3 have
been drawn from the originals by Mr William Gibb].

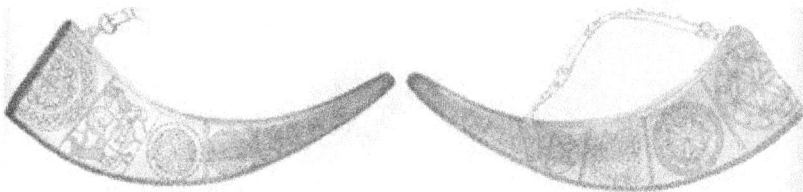

2

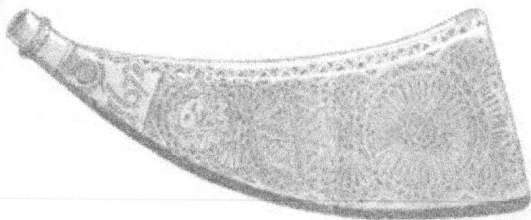

3

PLATE XXVI.—PISTOLS

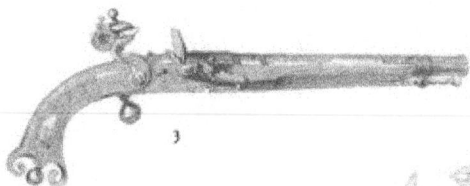

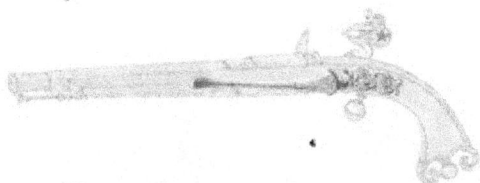

PLATE XXVII.—PISTOLS

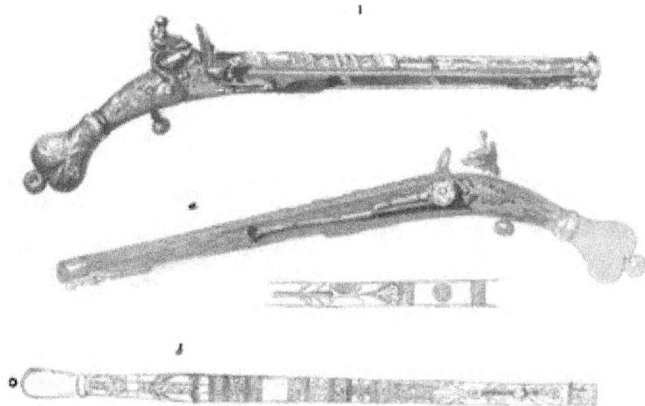

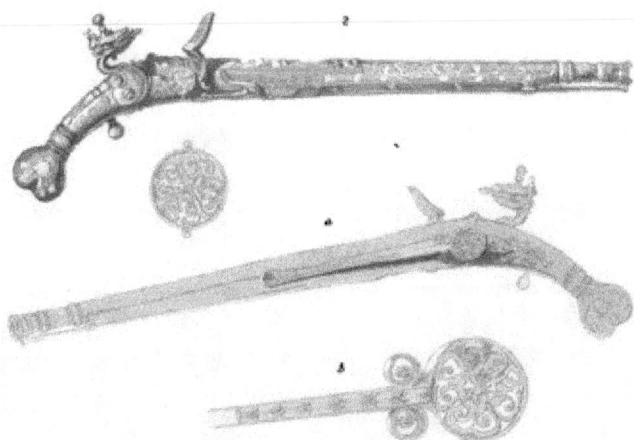

PLATE XXVIII.—PISTOLS

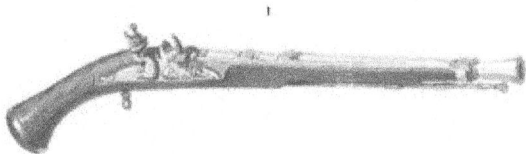

1

2

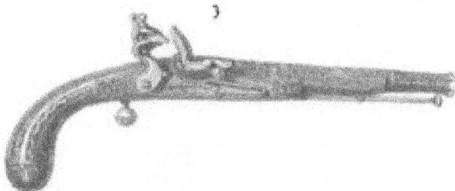

3

4

5

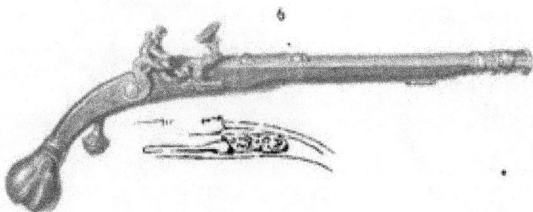

6

PLATE XXIX.—MUSKETS

Fig.

MUSKET, with flint-lock of early form, and ball trigger, the butt of the stock 1 fluted and ornamented with carved work, and inlaid with a marginal band of a running scroll of foliageous ornament.

MUSKET, with flint-lock of early form, the butt of the stock fluted, and carved with a fern- 2 leaf pattern.

MUSKET, 5 feet 4 inches in length, with flint-lock of early form, and lengthened trigger- 3 guard, the barrel finished with an ornamental muzzle; the stock fluted and inlaid with a hunting scene in mother of pearl. On the barrel is engraved the inscription :—

DOMINVS IOHANNES GRANT MILES VICECOMES DE INNERNES ME FECIT IN GERMANIA ANNO 1434.

and in an oval, three crowns with the letters S. I. G. and the words OF FREUCHY on a band round the margin. The date thus ascribed to the piece (as it now exists) cannot possibly be correct.

MUSKET, 5 feet 3 inches in length, with flint-lock of early form and lengthened trigger- 4 guard, the stock beautifully ornamented with foliageous scroll work.

CARBINE, 3 feet 5½ inches in length, with flint-lock, the barrel bell-mouthed at the muzzle; 5 the stock fluted.

MUSKET, wanting lock, 5 feet 8¾ inches in length.

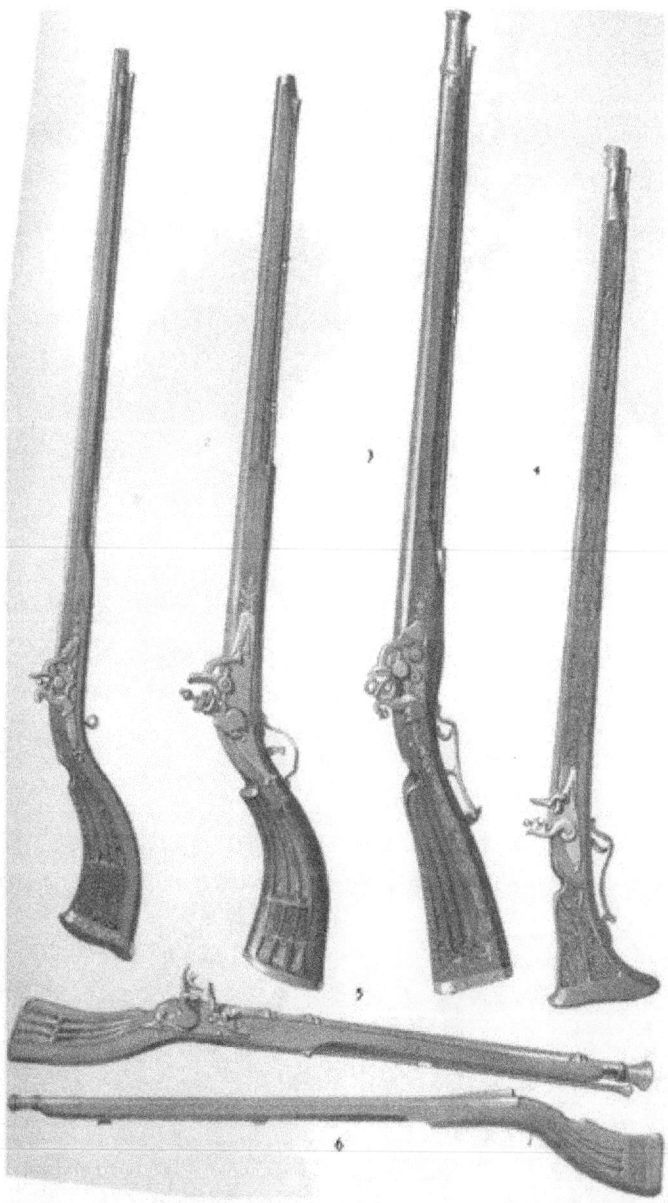

PLATE XXX.—MUSKETS

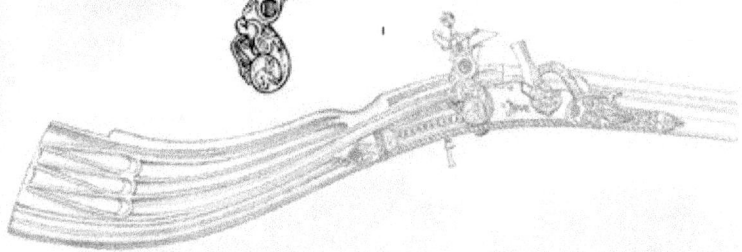

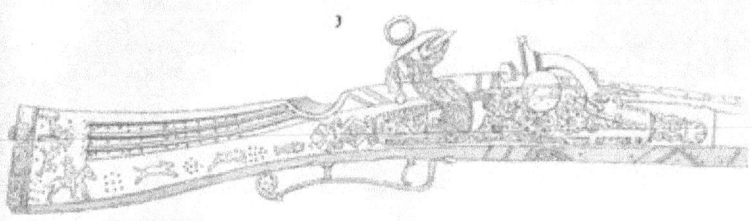

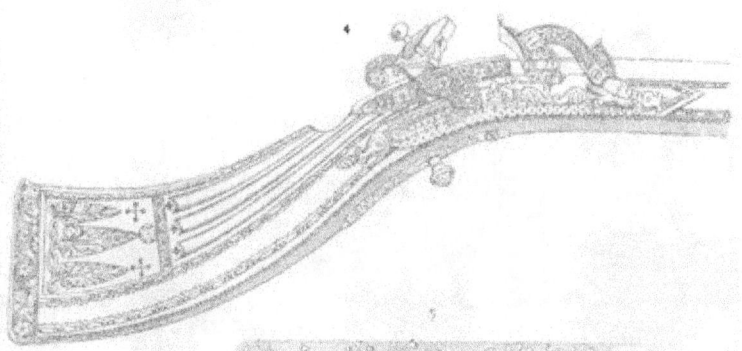

PLATE XXXI.—GLAIVES

GLAIVE, with hand-guard and blade of unusual length, measuring 3 feet from butt to 1
point, nearly two-thirds of which project beyond the pole, to which it is secured by a
collar, the back of which is prolonged as a strap down the back of the pole to the hand-
guard, and fastened at intervals with studs. The butt of the blade is similarly prolonged
into a strap, reaching down the front of the pole to the hand-guard. In the possession
of the Earl of Cawdor.

GLAIVE, similar but smaller, with hand-guard. In the possession of Lord Seafield. Two 2
almost similar specimens are in the collection of Sir J. Noel Paton, Kt., R.S.A., and
are thus described in the "Private Catalogue" (1879) of that collection : "Nos, 215, 216.
Two extremely rare and remarkable Glaives, with hand-guard, bearing considerable
resemblance to weapons represented in Continental illuminations of the 15th Century,
but held by Mr Drummond, R.S.A., to be undoubtedly Highland. There is another
in this collection, No. 541, 15th Century. From Murthly Castle."

BILL, 2 feet 9 inches in length from the collar of the socket to the point of the upper part 3
of the blade, deeply indented, and the point thrown forward, the back of the blade
prolonged into a stout end-spike, 12 inches in length, and a short, straight back-spike,
3½ inches long in the middle of the blade, which is carried on the pole by an open
socket 9 inches in length, and prolonged in straps down the front and back. A
weapon similar to this, but wanting the straps on the pole, is in the possession of Sir
Charles Forbes, Bart.

BILL of peculiar form, the blade scythe-shaped, with an end-spike starting from the forward 4
curve of the back of the blade, and no back-spike.

GLAIVE of peculiar form, with broad blade carried on the long, slender, flattened shank of 5
the socket, and pierced near the back by an elongated opening.

GLAIVE of peculiar form, approaching nearly to that of the Lochaber Axe. 6

GLAIVE, in form resembling a long knife-blade, fixed on the end of the pole by its tang, 7
and the pole strengthened by a collar.

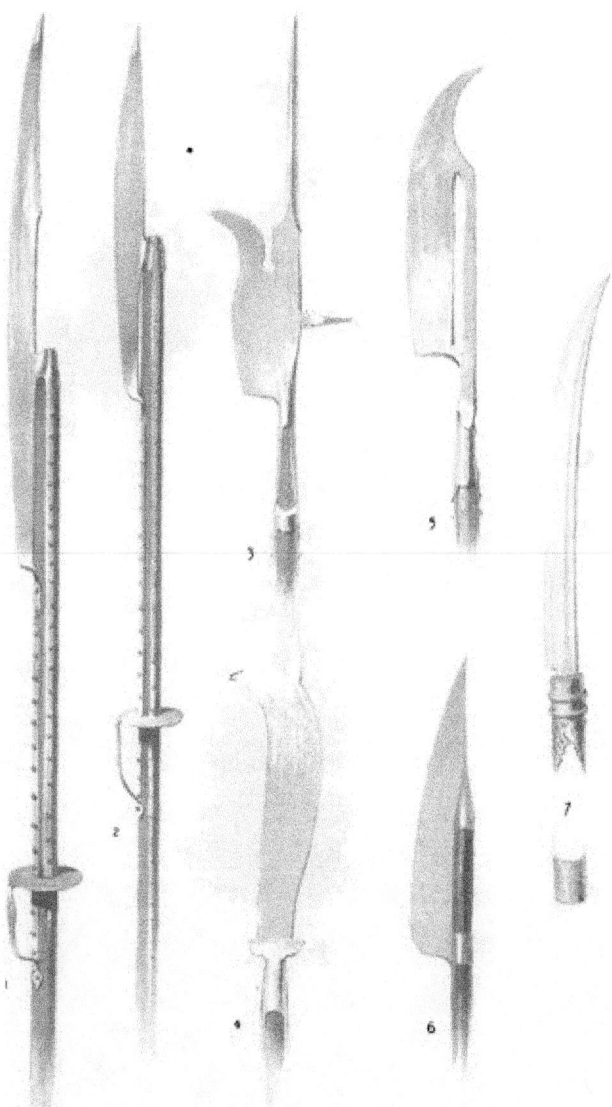

1   2   3   5   4   6   7

PLATE XXXII.—LOCHABER AXES

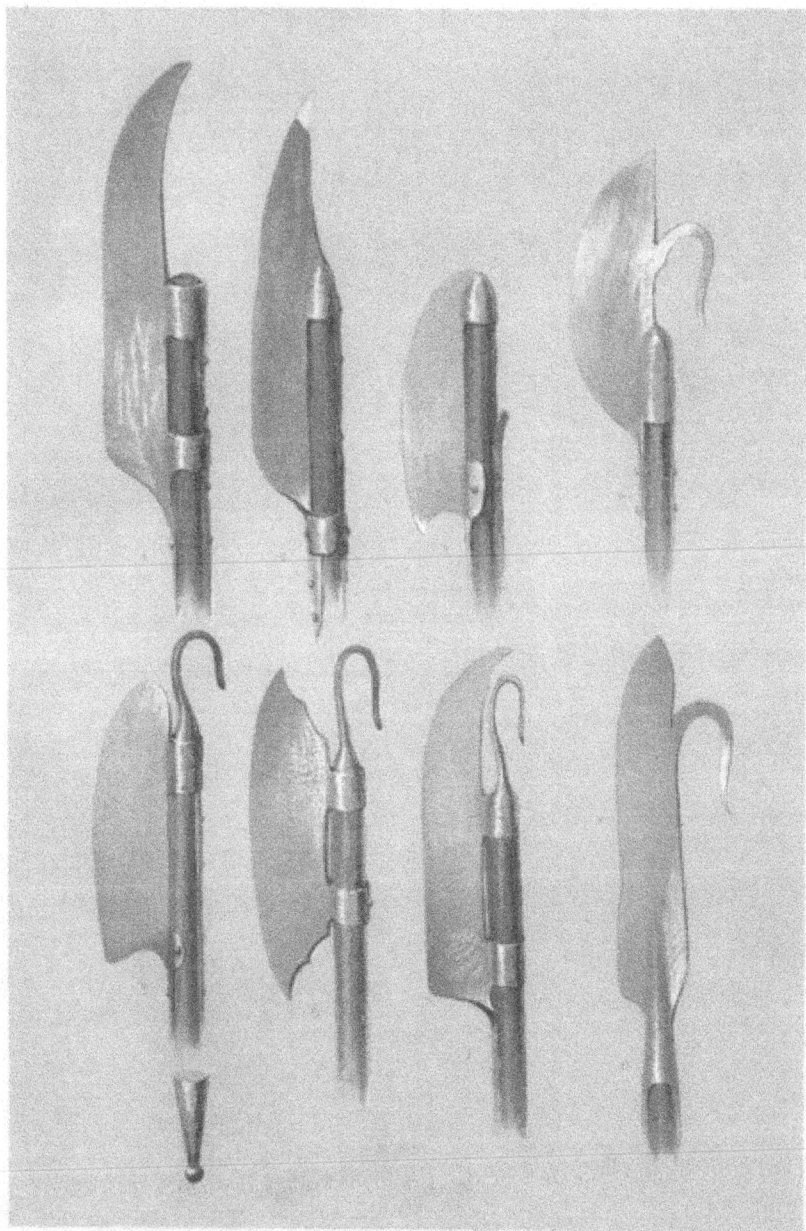

PLATE XXXIII.—HALBARDS, &c.

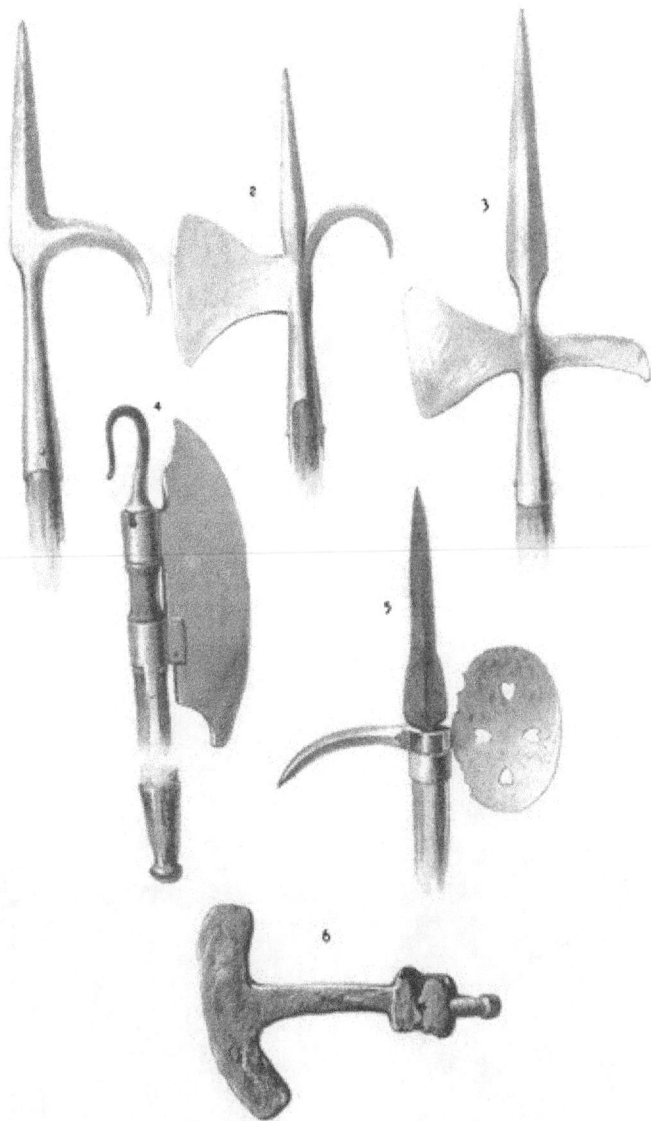

PLATE XXXIV.—WAR AXES

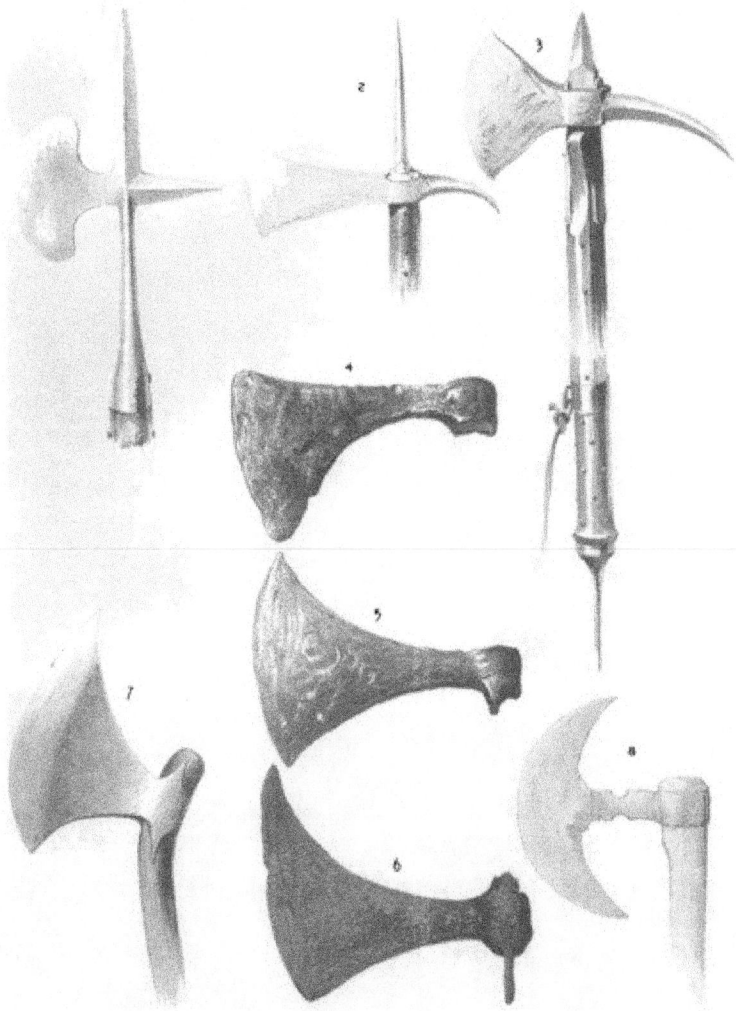

PLATE XXXV.—HALBARDS

Fig

H ALBARD, having a broad leaf-shaped head, small axe with concave edge, and 1
double back-spike; the head carried by a short socket with long straps on front
and back of the pole.

HALBARD, having a broad pike-shaped head, axe with convex edge, and broad recurved 2
back-spike; the head carried on a long tapering socket.

HALBARD, having a broad pike-shaped head, axe crescent-shaped, and broad recurved 3
back-spike.

PARTIZAN, with broad straight-edged blade and double wings; the head carried on a stout 4
socket with triple mountings.

PLATE XXXVI.—SPORRANS OR BELT PURSES

SPORRAN OR BELT-PURSE of dogskin, with tassel of leather, the mouth mounted   1
with hinged semi-circular clasps of silver, fastening with a spring lever and catch.
The Purse measures 6 inches in depth and 5 inches in width.   It formed part of
the collection of the late Mr James Drummond, R.S.A., bequeathed to the National
Museum of Antiquities, Edinburgh.

SPORRAN OR BELT-PURSE of leather, with tassel in front, and one at each side; the mouth   2
mounted with hinged semi-circular clasps of brass, ornamented with engraved circles
and dots, and closing with a spring lever and catch.

SPORRAN OR BELT-PURSE of doeskin, with mounting of white metal, ornamented with   3
scroll-work and female figures in relief, the knobs on the upper part chased as female
heads.   The bag is ornamented with a rosette in the centre, and a chevrony pattern
round the margin.

SPORRAN OR BELT-PURSE of sealskin, with tassel of twisted thong, the mouth mounted   4
with heavy flat-topped clasps of brass, closing with a spring lever and catch, and
ornamented with concentric circles and central dots.   Bequeathed by Mr Drummond
to the National Museum of Antiquities, Edinburgh.

SPORRAN OR BELT-PURSE of doeskin, with semi-circular clasps of iron, with ornamental   5
knobs of grotesque heads of animals.   It measures 12¼ inches in depth and 9¾ inches
in width, and opens by sliding the ornamental heads on the clasp.   It formed part of the
collection of the late Mr Drummond, and was acquired at the sale of that collection by
Mr P. Mortimer, London.

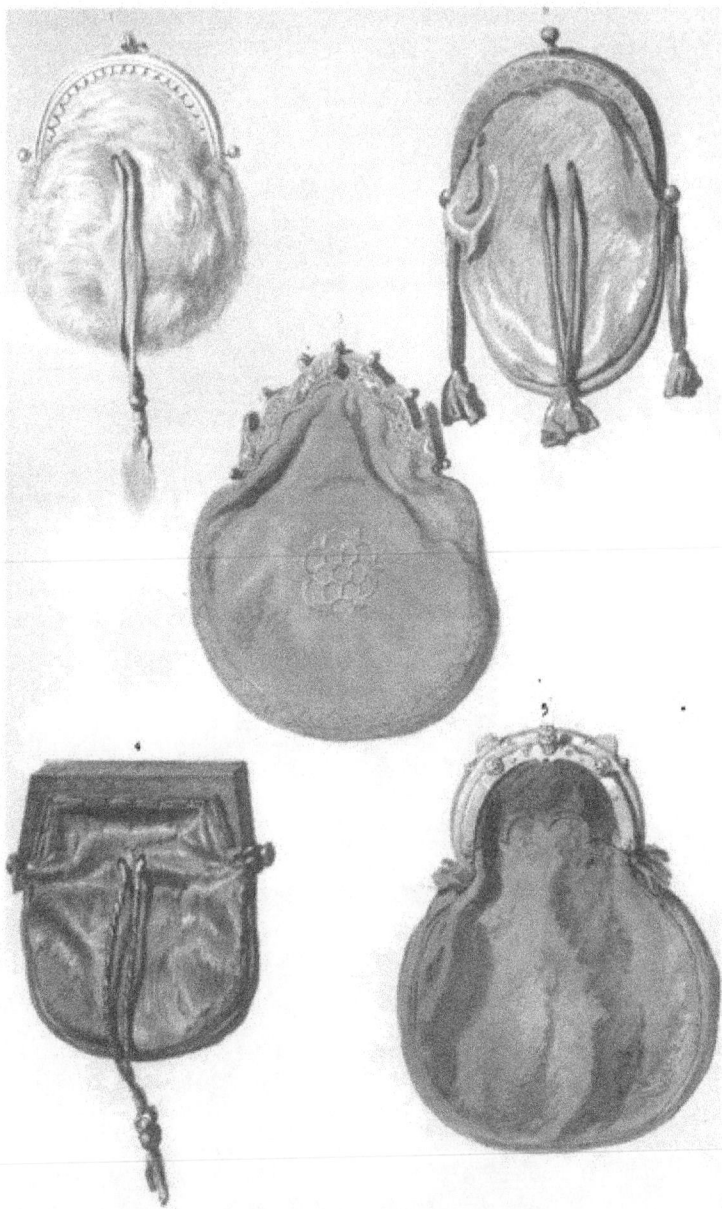

PLATE XXXVII.—SPORRANS AND PURSE CLASPS

Fig.

SPORRAN, with three long looped tassels, having a semicircular clasp of metal, 1 ornamented with a row of engraved concentric circles with central dots, mounted on a fringe of scarlet cloth, and closing with a spring lever and catch, with a button at top.

SPORRAN, with five short tassels, having a semicircular clasp of metal, ornamented with a 2 row of small engraved circles with central dots, and closing with a spring lever and catch, with a button at top.

SPORRAN, OR BELT-PURSE of doeskin, closing with a flap of the same material instead of a 3 clasp, and ornamented with three tags and tassels in front.

SPORRAN, OR BELT-PURSE CLASP of brass, flat-topped, and ornamented with studs and 4 circles, connected by opposing arcs of circles.

SPORRAN, OR BELT-PURSE CLASP of brass, ornamented with studs and circles, alternating 5 with heart-shaped openings, showing a lining of red cloth. The drawing shows the manner in which the hinges are made to work on two round-beaded pins.

BELT-PURSE CLASP of brass, with ring and sliding loop for the belt, ornamented with 6 engraved scrolls.

SPORRAN, OR BELT-PURSE CLASP of brass, pentagonal in form, and ornamented with con- 7 centric circles and central dots.

SPORRAN, OR BELT-PURSE CLASP of brass, semicircular in form, and finely ornamented 8 with a wavy foliageous scroll; the alternate branches of which enclose circular spaces filled with punctuations.

SPORRAN, OR BELT-PURSE CLASP of brass, semicircular in form, decorated with an engraved 9 border of vandyke ornament and a row of concentric circles with central dots.

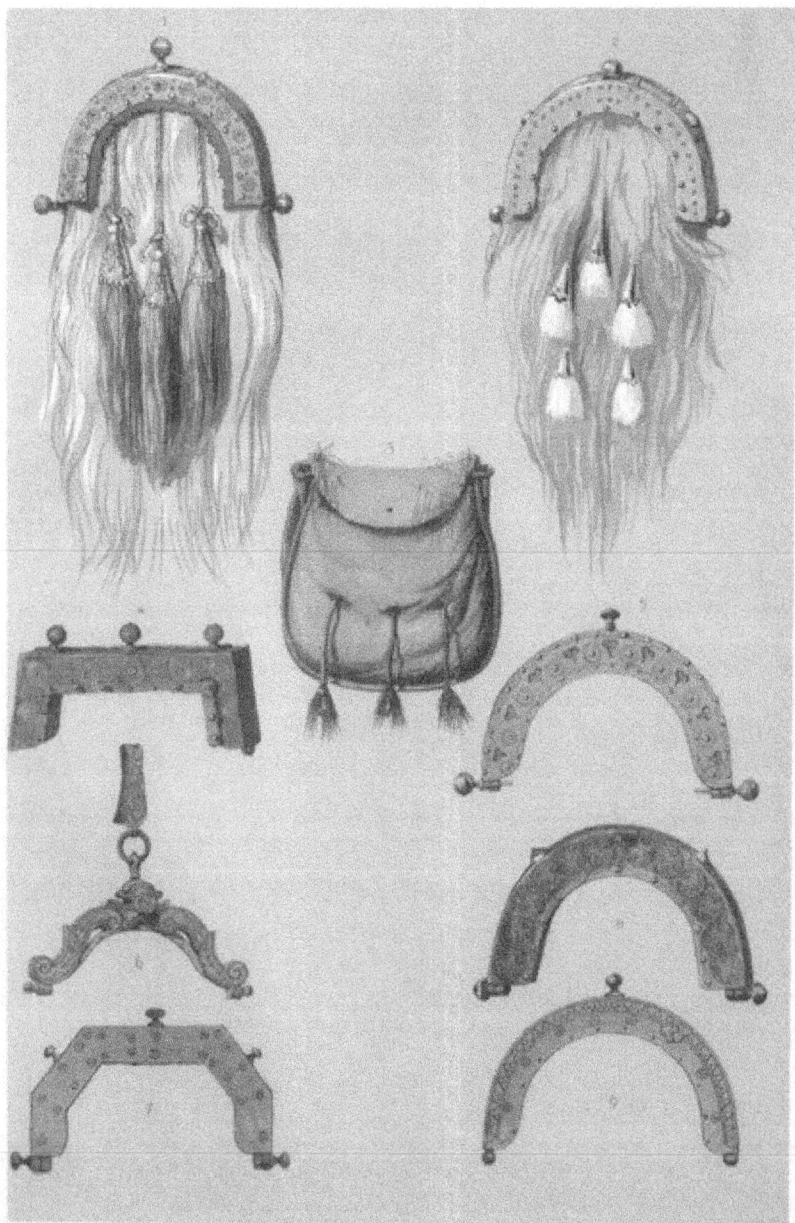

PLATE XXXVIII.—SPORRANS **AND PURSE CLASPS**

Fig

SPORRAN, OR BELT-PURSE CLASP of brass, semi-circular in form, and orna- 1
mented by a peculiar division of the surface into triangular and quadrangular
spaces filled with engraved lines, sometimes parallel, sometimes cross-hatched. Two of
the larger spaces contain a star of five points within a pentagonal figure; the central
star and figure are hexagonal, and the central divisions of the two next it are filled
with rosettes.

SPORRAN, OR BELT-PURSE CLASP of brass, flat-topped, having in the centre of the front a 2
crown dividing the initials W. W., and on either side a thistle and scroll. Round the
inner margin is engraved the distich :—

> "OPEN MY MOUTH, CUT NOT MY SKIN,
> AND THEN YOU'LL SEE WHAT IS THEREIN."

This specimen is preserved in the Museum at Elgin.

SPORRAN, OR BELT-PURSE of sealskin, with leather loop for the belt; the mouth covered 3
with a fringed flap of metal, ornamented with three stars and a rose and thistle
crowned; the front ornamented with six looped tassels. Bequeathed to the National
Museum of Antiquities, Edinburgh, by the late Mr Drummond, R.S.A.

SPORRAN, OR BELT-PURSE of sealskin, 6¼ inches wide and 8 inches deep, with semi-circular 4
clasp of brass, ornamented with pierced heart-shaped spaces lined with scarlet cloth;
the front ornamented with a single long tag and tassel. Bequeathed to the National
Museum of Antiquities, Edinburgh, by the late Mr Drummond, R.S.A.

SPORRAN, OR BELT-PURSE of doeskin, with semi-circular clasp of brass, ornamented with 5
an engraved wavy foliageous scroll; the front and sides adorned with knotted tags
and tassels of leather. This peculiar specimen is in the collection of Sir J. Noel
Paton, Kt., R.S.A., and is thus described in the Private Catalogue of that collection :—
"Highland Sporran of great beauty, and in perfect and pristine condition. It has no
metal catches for belt, but has been suspended by a leather loop, which remains. The
clasp, of brass, is beautifully engraved with a Celto-Gothic scroll and border. On the top
of the clasp the date 1724 is engraved in a style much later than the ornamentation. This
sporran was considered by the late Mr Drummond (who made a beautiful drawing of it)
one of the earliest and finest he had ever met with. *From Brahan Castle.*"

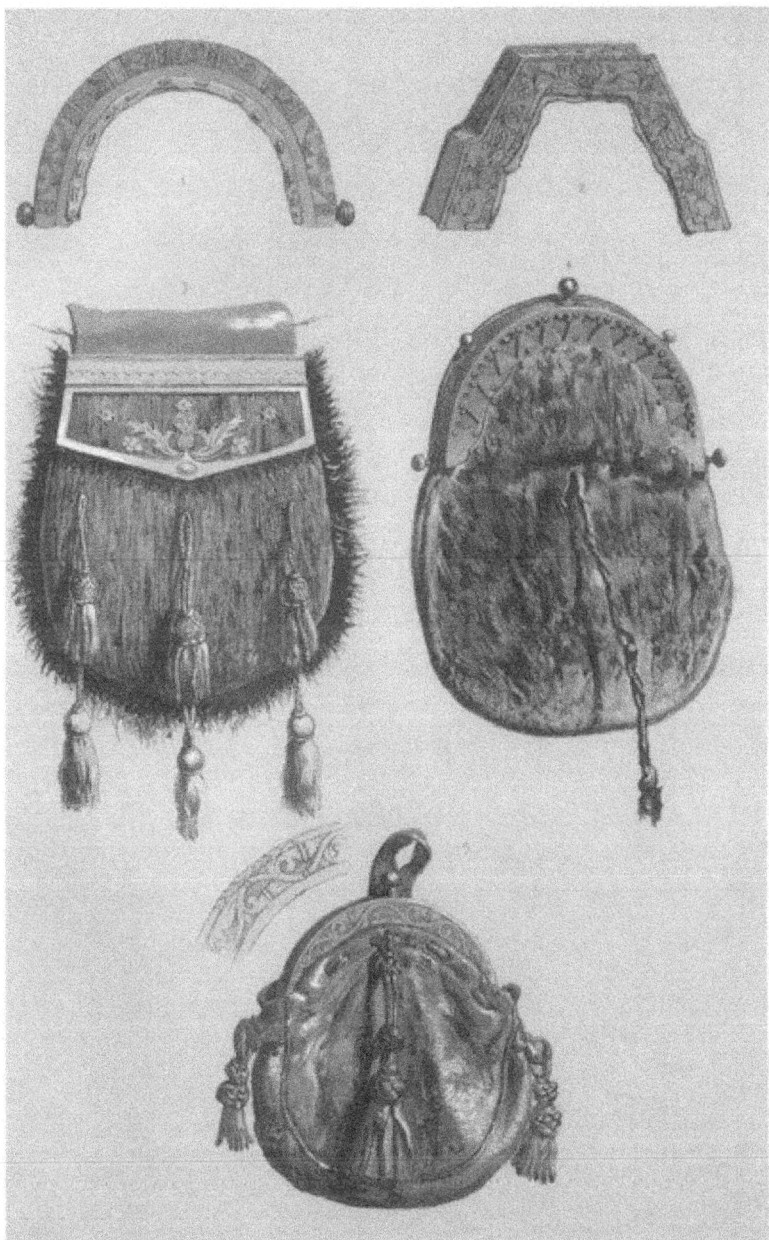

PLATE XXXIX.—POUCHES

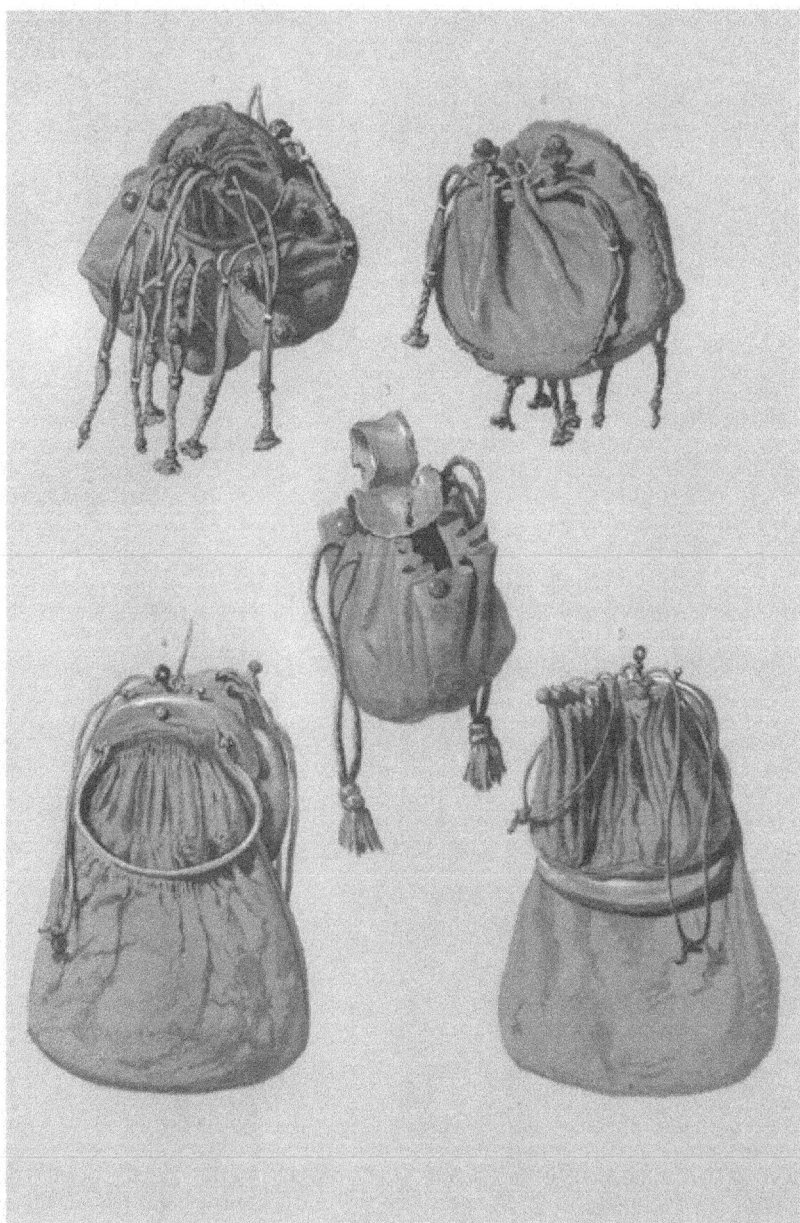

PLATE XL.—BROOCHES

HIGHLAND BROOCH OF BRASS, 6 inches diameter, ornamented with pierced 1
borders and patterns of interlaced work and foliage. Four circles of the same
diameter as the width from the outer to the inner border of the brooch are placed at
equal distances, each filled with a different pattern of complicated interlaced work,
surrounded by a pierced border enclosed within a band of engraved parallel lines. The
segmental spaces between the circles are filled with foliage delicately outlined on a
ground of cross-hatched lines, and pierced with five circular apertures. The pin is of
the flattened quadrangular form, with the expanded ornamental head usually found in
these brooches, and is let into a narrow slit cut out of the body of the brooch from
either side to near the centre. The head of the pin has a slit cut in it down to the
hole that receives the part of the brooch not cut away, and being thus pushed into
its place, the slit is closed and the pin works freely as on a hinge. This brooch is
in the collection of Sir J. Noel Paton, Kt., R.S.A., &c.

REVERSE OF THE SAME BROOCH, the circles similarly decorated with interlaced work; the 2
segmental places plain, with one exception, which has a sort of quatrefoil outlined on
a hatched ground.

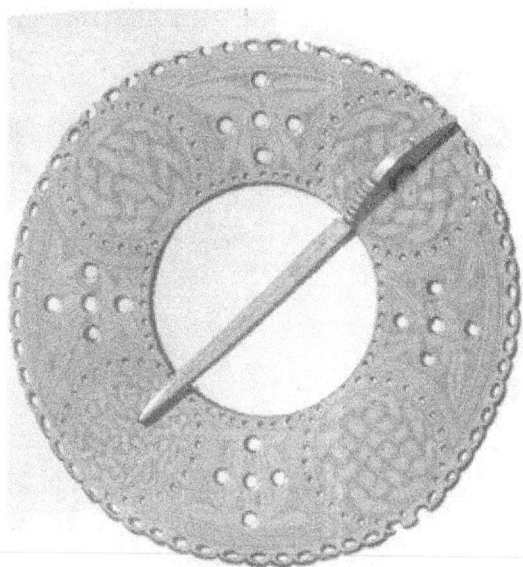

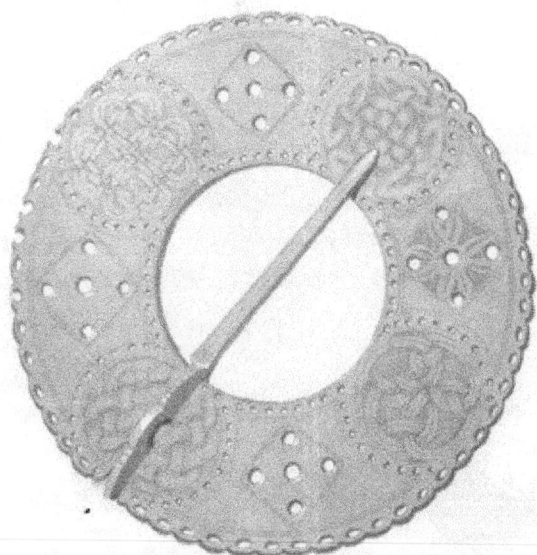

PLATE XLI.—BROOCHES

Highland Brooch of Brass, 5 inches diameter, ornamented with an 1
arcaded pattern, filled with bands of engraved parallel lines set obliquely to each
other, and the spaces above and between the arcs engraved with a rude imitation of
foliage. The pin is of the form usually seen in these brooches.

Flattened Ring of Brass of Oval Form, ornamented with a series of double triangles 2
set point to point.

Highland Brooch of Brass, 6 inches in diameter, boldly ornamented with engraved 3
borders; circles of interlaced work and foliage. The circular spaces, six in number,
are filled with different patterns of interlaced work, and the segmental spaces between
them with quaintly designed patterns of a foliageous character. In one of these,
instead of foliage, the artist has introduced an animal apparently biting its own back.
The pin of this brooch is not flattened transversely to the head as is the usual form.

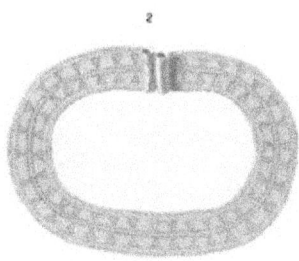

PLATE XLII.—BROOCHES

HIGHLAND BROOCH OF BRASS, finely decorated with engraved borders enclos-   1
ing a running pattern of a wavy foliageous scroll, delicately outlined on a ground
of cross-hatched lines. The pin is of the usual form, but presents the unusual feature
of being ornamented with a kind of simple fret. A brooch of slightly smaller size,
precisely similar in pattern, but having no fret on the pin, is in the National Museum
of Antiquities, Edinburgh.

HIGHLAND BROOCH OF BRASS, boldly but rudely ornamented with circles and foliage in   2
the interspaces. The pin is of iron and more slender than usual. This brooch is in
the National Museum of Antiquities, Edinburgh. It was found in Canisbay Moor,
Caithness.

HIGHLAND BROOCH OF BRASS, ornamented with borders of engraved lines, enclosing circles   3
of interlaced work and foliage in the interspaces. The circles are filled with complicated
interlacements. Two of the interspaces are filled with foliage. One of the other two
is divided into three triangles, one of which is filled by a triquetra. In the remaining
interspace between the circles is the figure of a lion-like animal rather spiritedly
rendered.

HIGHLAND BROOCH OF BRASS, curiously ornamented in compartments of a chevrony pattern   4
of triangles, alternately plain and filled with parallel lines. Between each two of
these compartments is one which simulates a black-letter inscription. The letters are not
real letters, but mere ornamental markings. The brooch has been mended at the hinge
of the pin, and the manner in which the mended piece has been riveted on is shown by a
diagram over the drawing.

PLATE XLIII.—BROOCHES

HIGHLAND BROOCH OF BRASS, 6 inches diameter, boldly decorated with 1 borders of engraved lines and patterns of interlaced work and foliage. Five circles are placed at equal distances round the ring of the brooch. Of these two are filled with interlaced work surrounded by a border of zig-zags, apparently intended for leaflets. Two others are filled with floral devices. The fifth, which is cut in the centre for the insertion of the pin, is rudely filled with cross bands. The interspaces between the circles are all filled with foliage, or attempts to represent foliage, except one, which shows the figure of an animal. The pin of this brooch is longer than usual, and presents the further peculiarity of being ornamented with a kind of running pattern of a plait of two strands.

HIGHLAND BROOCH OF BRASS, simply decorated with a chevrony pattern, each alternate 2 triangle filled with parallel lines. This brooch is in the National Museum of Antiquities, Edinburgh. It was found at Uidh, in the island of Taransay, Harris.

HIGHLAND BROOCH OF BRASS, wanting the pin, and rudely ornamented with circles and 3 other patterns nearly obliterated by wear. In the National Museum of Antiquities, Edinburgh.

SMALL HIGHLAND BROOCH OF BRASS, wanting the pin, and ornamented with segmental 4 patterns filled with engraved parallel lines.

SMALL HIGHLAND BROOCH OF BRASS, very rudely ornamented with engraved designs of 5 irregular character. The pin of this brooch is of iron, round and tapering to a sharp point, thus differing from the pins commonly found in these brooches.

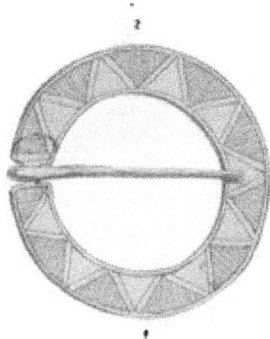

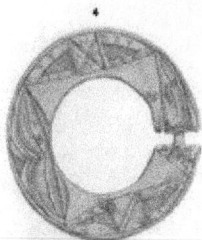

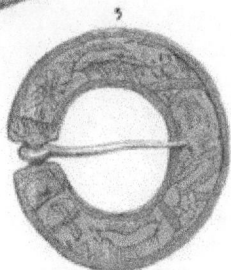

PLATE XLIV.—BROOCHES

Fig.

HIGHLAND BROOCH OF SILVER, circular in form, inlaid with niello, and 1
ornamented with engraved circular patterns of chequered work, and foliage filling
the spaces between the patterns outlined in niello. The pin is of the form which has
a longitudinal slit in the upper part of the head for the passage of the bar on which
it plays.

HIGHLAND BROOCH OF SILVER, circular in form, and richly engraved with circular patterns of 2
interlaced work and foliage. The external outline of the brooch is diversified by the
projection of parts of the patterns, giving it a more highly ornamental form. The pin
is of the modern form, attached by a hinge and catch at the back of the brooch.

HIGHLAND BROOCH OF BRASS, circular in form, and richly engraved with circular patterns of 3
interlaced work and floral ornament. The spaces between the circles are filled with
scrolls and grotesque figures of animals, with punctulated ornamentation. The pin is
wanting.

HIGHLAND BROOCH OF BRASS, circular in form, ornamented with an imbricated pattern 4
arranged as a six-rayed star, with floral forms in the spaces between the points. The
pin tapers from head to point, and wants the usual slit in the upper part of the head.

ANCIENT CELTIC BROOCH OF SILVER, penannular in form, with extremely long pin. 5

ANCIENT CELTIC BROOCH, with long pin, the head of which is looped on the ring of the 6
brooch.

ANCIENT CELTIC BROOCH, penannular in form, with zig-zag ornament, and two sockets for 7
settings; the pin round and tapering and of great length.

3

4

A R
CMD-1710

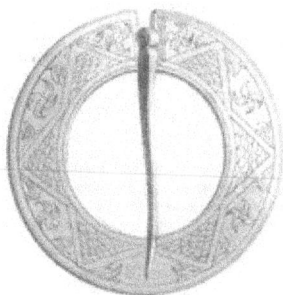

5

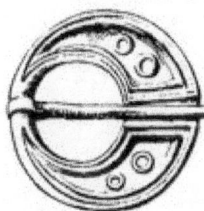

7

6

PLATE XLV.—LUCKENBOOTH BROOCHES

PLATE XLVI.—BROOCH AND CHARM STONE

BROOCH, silver gilt, 5¼ inches in greatest diameter, in the centre a large circular   1
setting of rock-crystal, round which is inscribed the distich :—

DE ● SERVE AND HAIF

THE ● HEVEN ● BABAIF.

The expanded border is divided into eight compartments, each filled with the same
pattern of scroll ornament as that on the opposite side. Two of these compartments are
inscribed with the letters M.C., and are otherwise without ornament. Two bear shields
with the gyronny of the Campbells in the first and fourth quarters, the second and
third blank. The other compartments are filled with foliageous scroll ornament. This
brooch has been long in the possession of the Campbells of Ballochyle, Holyloch,
Cowall, Argyleshire. Probably on account of its rock-crystal setting, it was regarded
as a charm against disease and witchcraft.

SIDE VIEW OF THE BROOCH, showing its elevation.   2

VIEW OF THE BACK OF THE BROOCH, showing the pin with its hinge and catch.   3

THE CLACH DEARG; a ball of rock-crystal, in a mounting of two hoops of silver, with a   4
loop for suspension. It has been long in the possession of the Stewarts of Ardvoirlich,
and was formerly held in great repute in the neighbourhood as a charm-stone for
curing diseases of cattle.

PLATE XLVII.—BAGPIPES

Fig

HIGHLAND BAGPIPE, having two small drones and chanter, finely ornamented with Celtic patterns carved in circular bands. The drones are inserted in a stock apparently formed from a forked branch, the fork giving the drones their proper spread for the shoulder. In the centre of the stock are the letters R M'D, below them a galley, and below the galley is the date in Roman numerals, M : CCCC : IX. The date is shown enlarged in Fig. 7. The letters, both in the initials above the galley and in the numeral inscription, are of the Gothic form commonly used in the fifteenth century. On the reverse of the stock (shown in Fig. 2) is a triplet of foliageous scroll-work. Bands of interlaced work encircle the ends of the forked part, which are bound with brass ferrules. The lower joint of one of the drones is ornamented with a band of interlaced work in the centre. The corresponding joint of the other drone is not original. The upper joints of the drones are ornamented with two bands of interlaced work, and terminate in cup-shaped heads, each of which is also ornamented with a band of interlaced work. The chanter is ornamented at both extremities with interlaced work, and the finger-holes, seven in number, are greatly worn. An enlarged diagram of the ornament on the upper part of the chanter is given as Fig. 3. The nail-heads placed round the lower part of the bell of the chanter are decorated with engraved ornament. An enlarged diagram of the carved interlaced work on the bell and the engraved ornament of the studs is given as Fig. 4. The bag and blow-pipe of the instrument are modern. This unique stand of bagpipes is in the possession of Mr Robert Glen, Musical Instrument Maker, Edinburgh.

Reverse side of the stock, showing its ornament. 2

Ornament round the upper part of the chanter. 3

Ornament on the bell of the chanter and engraved ornament on its brass studs. 4

Ornament on one of the brass ferrules of the drone. 5

Ornament on another of the brass ferrules of the drone. 6

Enlarged copy of the Gothic numerals forming the date carved in relief on the stock. 7

CALABRIAN BAGPIPE, used in Italy for playing an accompaniment to the pipe. It has four drones in one stock, the longest 3 feet in length, the stock being 8 inches long. This specimen, which seems to be of the last century, is also in the possession of Mr Robert Glen.

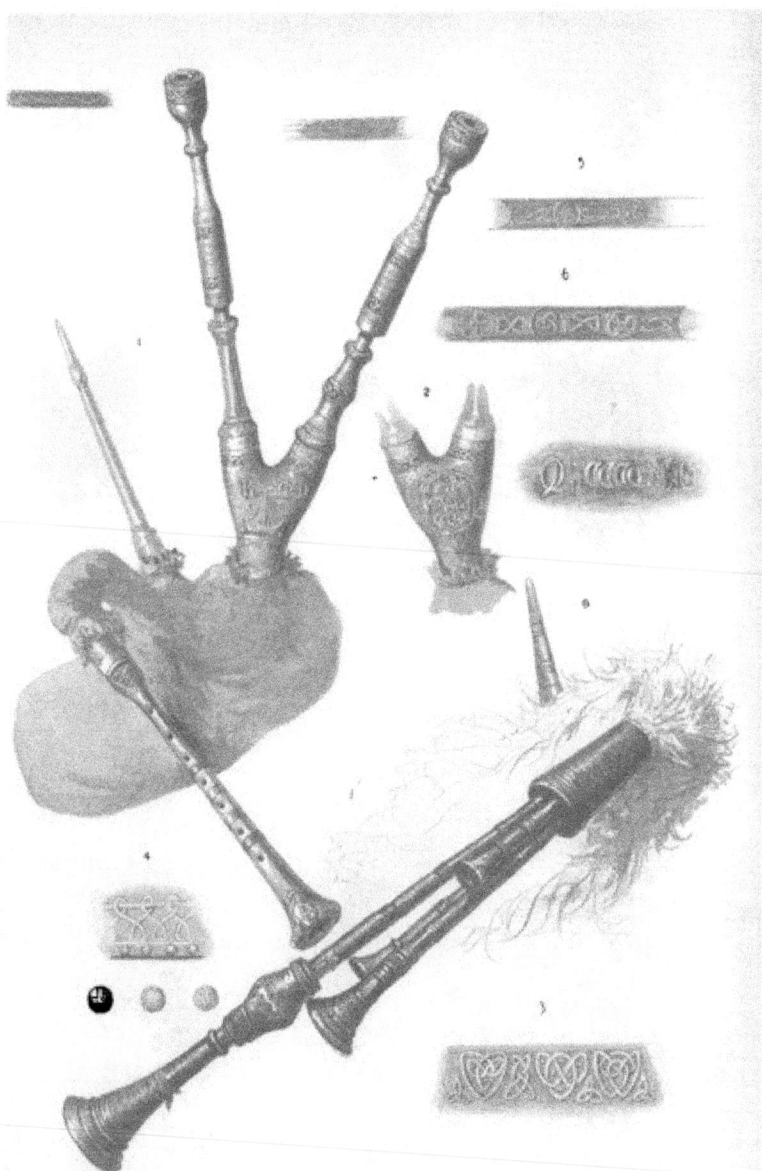

PLATE XLVIII.—THE "QUEEN MARY" HARP

SCOTTISH HARP, measuring 31 inches in extreme length, and 18 inches in extreme width. It consists of three parts, the body or box of the instrument, in front of which is the sounding-board, with the pins in the string-holes, the comb or upper arm with the stretching pins, and the bow or fore-arm of the instrument richly ornamented. The body of the harp, or box, is of willow wood, hollowed out of the solid. It measures 27 inches in length, 12 inches in width at the base, tapering to 5 inches at the top, and 4¼ inches in depth throughout. The front or sounding-board of the box rises in the centre from both ends and from each side. The central ridge is pierced by twenty-nine pin-holes, and there is a loop at the bottom for the thirtieth string. The holes are encircled on the upper sides by horse-shoe shaped mountings of brass. The pins are round-headed. The panels on either side of the central ridge are ornamented with a central circle enclosing an equal armed cross. Above and below the central circles are bands placed saltire-wise, with four sounding holes at the intersections, and a Latin cross in the wide angle of the saltires at the lower end. The sides of the box are similarly ornamented. The comb or upper arm projects 14¼ inches beyond the box, being oval in section towards the junction with the top of the box, and triangular towards the forward end. It is pierced for thirty strings, and the stretching pins remain in the holes. Its ornamentation is in a similar style to that of the body of the harp. The bow or fore-arm is 23 inches in length along the inner curve, rising 4 inches from the chord. Its termination below the box of the harp is boldly carved into the form of an animal's head, and the rounded front of the arm is similarly treated, and finely ornamented with foliageous scrolls in relief. Six silver studs are inserted in the plain part between the scrolls. The sides of the bow are also ornamented with foliageous scrolls of great beauty, engraved in the wood and stained. At the upper and lower ends are circular spaces enclosing figures of nondescript animals. The inner edge of the bow is decorated with a running pattern of interlaced work engraved and stained. The details of the ornament are given on an enlarged scale on Plate XLIX. This harp, which was long in the family of the Robertsons of Lude, has been deposited for exhibition in the National Museum of Antiquities by John Steuart, Esq. of Dalguise, the present representative of the family. It is traditionally said to have been given by Queen Mary to Beatrix Garden, by whom it was brought to Lude on her marriage with a member of the Robertson family.

[Advantage has been taken of the presence of the harp in the Museum to verify the drawing, and to complete the details of the ornament.]

PLATE XLIX.—ORNAMENT OF "QUEEN MARY" HARP

Fig.

ORNAMENT of the upper part of right side of the bow or fore-arm of the "Queen Mary" harp, consisting of interlaced foliageous scrolls, and a medallion enclosing a leonine animal, partially defaced. — 1

ORNAMENT of the lower part of right side of the bow or fore-arm of the harp, consisting of interlaced foliageous scrolls, and a medallion enclosing a group of three animals—a horse, and a nondescript beast swallowing a fish. — 2

ORNAMENT of the upper part of the front of the box or sounding-board of the harp, immediately under its junction with the upper arm, consisting of a symmetrical pattern of foliageous scroll-work. — 3

ORNAMENT of the front of the bow, immediately under the triangular termination of the upper arm of the harp, consisting of a symmetrical pattern of foliageous scroll-work. — 4

ORNAMENT of upper part of left side of the bow or fore-arm of the harp, consisting of foliageous scroll-work and a medallion enclosing a winged griffin. — 5

ORNAMENT of the lower part of left side of the bow or fore-arm of the harp, consisting of foliageous scrolls and a medallion enclosing a cockatrice. — 6

ORNAMENT of the lower part of the inner edge of the bow of the harp, consisting of a running pattern of interlaced work. — 7

ORNAMENT of the upper part of the inner edge of the bow of the harp, consisting of a running pattern of interlaced work. — 8

[These details of the ornament of the harp have been drawn from the original by Mr William Gibb.]

PLATE L.—THE LAMONT HARP

THIS HARP, which has been long known as the CLARSHACH LUMANACH, or Lamont Harp, in the family traditions of the Robertsons of Lude, is said to have been preserved in that family since 1464, when it is supposed to have been brought from Argyleshire by a daughter of the Lamont family on her marriage with one of the Robertsons.

Its extreme length is 38 inches, and its extreme width, from front to back, 18½ inches. The body of the instrument, or sounding box, is 30 inches in length, 4 inches in breadth at the top, and 17 inches at the bottom; the depth of the sides throughout being 4 inches, and the front rising in the centre with a swell of about 1 inch. The band down the centre is pierced by thirty-two string-holes. These have each an ornamental mounting of brass of peculiar form, except the three upper and two lower holes, which have mountings of horse-shoe shape terminating in quatrefoils. The upper arm of the harp is strengthened by a metal bar on each side pierced by thirty-two pin-holes, corresponding to the number of string-holes. All the pins are in position except two, although only a few are shown in the drawing. The triangular end of the upper arm is faced with a mounting of brass, having a plain oval projection in the centre, and the margin ornamented with engraved patterns, partly of a foliageous and partly of geometrical character. The bow of the harp measures along the chord of its arc 28 inches, and curves with a rise of 6¼ inches. It measures 3½ inches in width, 1½ inches in thickness, and the front expands to a width of 3½ inches. It is considerably warped, and its broken parts are fastened together by clamps of iron below and double clamps of brass above.

This harp was engraved and described as the "Caledonian Harp" in a treatise entitled, "An Historical Enquiry respecting the Performance on the Harp in the Highlands of Scotland," by Mr John Gunn, 4to, 1807. It has been recently deposited for exhibition in the National Museum of Antiquities, Edinburgh, by John Steuart, Esq., of Dalguise, the present representative of the family, and has been again figured and described by Mr Charles D. Bell, F.S.A. Scot., in the *Proceedings of the Society of Antiquaries of Scotland*, New Series, Vol. III. p. 10.

PLATE LI.—IRISH HARP

THIS IRISH HARP, formerly in the collection of the late Mr John Bell, Dungannon, is now in the National Museum of Antiquities, Edinburgh.

It measures in extreme length 3 feet 8½ inches, and in extreme width 2 feet 8½ inches. The body of the instrument, or sounding-box, measures 3 feet 2 inches in length, 3½ inches in breadth at the top, and 11 inches in breadth at the bottom, and is 3 inches deep throughout. The upper arm of the harp measures 27½ inches in extreme length, and terminates in front in the head of an animal. The fore-arm, or bow of the harp, measures 3 feet 10½ inches in length. The median line of the sounding-box is pierced for thirty-four strings, and the string-holes have triangular mountings of brass. The upper arm of the harp is strengthened by bars of metal on either side, pierced by holes for thirty-four pins. The sides of the body of the instrument are ornamented by a single wavy line carved in relief, and the six sounding holes are filled with a geometrical ornament.

PLATE LII.—METHERS OR DRINKING VESSELS

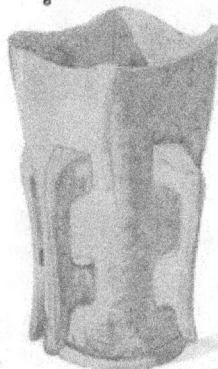

PLATE LIII.—SPADES

WOODEN SPADE, shod with iron, called a *ceaba*, from the island of Islay. It measures 5 feet 3 inches in total length, and differs from the ordinary spade in the projection of the blade to one side of the handle only. It is still in use as an ordinary implement of agriculture in Islay. The specimen from which the drawing is taken is in the National Museum of Antiquities, Edinburgh.   1

WOODEN SPADE, with long handle, slightly bent backwards, and terminating in a knob. The blade is triangular, and was probably shod with iron. The wood is oak; the length of the handle 3 feet 7 inches, length of the blade 10 inches, and its greatest breadth 5 inches. Found in an old coal-mine near Glasgow, and now in the National Museum of Antiquities, Edinburgh.   2

PEAT-SPADE, the lower end shod with iron, a spur for the foot projecting at one side of the lower end of handle; the upper end mounted with a horn.   3

DIVOT-SPADE, OR FLAUGHTER-SPADE, used for cutting "divots" or turf for building houses, or for weighting the thatch, or covering out-houses. It has a semi-circular blade, and a long and stout quadrangular handle with a cross-piece at the end, rounded at the extremities where it is grasped by the hands.   4

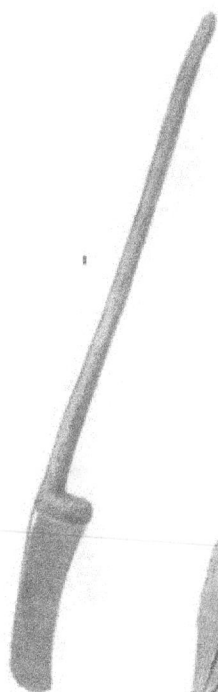

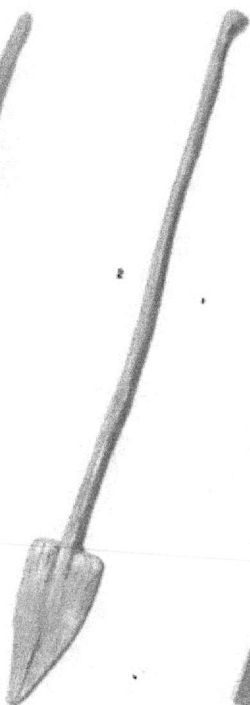

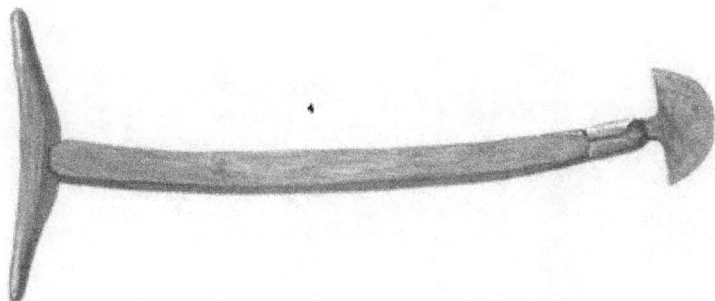

PLATE LIV.—IMPLEMENTS

MILITARY FLAIL, being a flail, with a short swingle-staff, bound with iron and 1
studded with spikes. The handle is 4 feet 9 inches in length; the swingle 1
foot 8¼ inches.

CASCHROM, a species of implement intermediate between the spade and the plough, used 2
for the tillage of rough ground on which a plough cannot be used with advantage.
It consists of a handle about 6 feet in length, fastened to a sole of about 3½ feet in
length, which is shod with an iron blade resembling that of a one-sided spade. A
pin projecting from the lower end of the handle gives a rest for the foot, by which
means the iron-shod part is driven into the ground, the long handle being used as
a lever to turn up the tilth.

SWYN-FEATHER, OR SWEDISH FEATHER, a kind of light and slender *rauteur* carried by 3
musketeers in the 16th century. It was often combined with the musket-rest, and
was used as a defence against cavalry.

SCOTTISH DISTAFF AND SPINDLE, with its stone whorl. The distaff was usually about 2 4
feet 6 inches in length, and the spindle about 12 inches in length. The lower part
of the distaff is ornamented with carved work. In the drawing the spindle is placed
in a perforation of the distaff through which the belt was passed to support it on the
side of the person spinning from it.

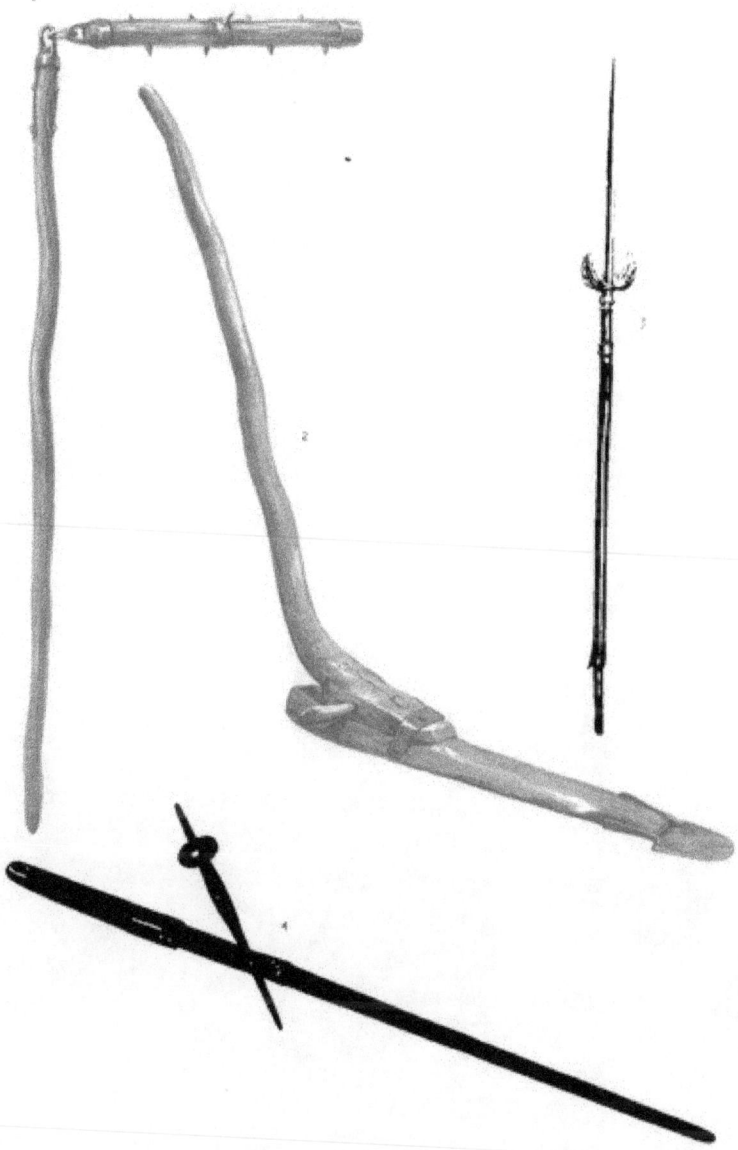

www.ingramcontent.com/pod-product-compliance
Lightning Source LLC
Chambersburg PA
CBHW020853270326
41928CB00006B/682